Women's Issues in Margaret Atwood's *The Handmaid's Tale*

Other Books in the Social Issues in Literature Series:

Social Issues
in Literature

Women's Issues in Margaret Atwood's *The Handmaid's Tale*

David E. Nelson, Book Editor

GREENHAVEN PRESS
A part of Gale, Cengage Learning

GALE
CENGAGE Learning·

Detroit • New York • San Francisco • New Haven, Conn • Waterville, Maine • London

GALE
CENGAGE Learning·

Elizabeth Des Chenes, *Managing Editor*

© 2012 Greenhaven Press, a part of Gale, Cengage Learning

Gale and Greenhaven Press are registered trademarks used herein under license.

For more information, contact:
Greenhaven Press
27500 Drake Rd.
Farmington Hills, MI 48331-3535
Or you can visit our Internet site at gale.cengage.com

For product information and technology assistance, contact us at

Gale Customer Support, 1-800-877-4253
For permission to use material from this text or product, submit all requests online at www.cengage.com/permissions

Further permissions questions can be emailed to permissionrequest@cengage.com

Articles in Greenhaven Press anthologies are often edited for length to meet page requirements. In addition, original titles of these works are changed to clearly present the main thesis and to explicitly indicate the author's opinion. Every effort is made to ensure that Greenhaven Press accurately reflects the original intent of the authors. Every effort has been made to trace the owners of copyrighted material.

Cover photograph copyright © KC Armstrong/Corbis.

LIBRARY OF CONGRESS CATALOGING-IN-PUBLICATION DATA

Women's issues in Margaret Atwood's The handmaid's tale / David E. Nelson, book editor.
p. cm. -- (Social issues in literature)
Includes bibliographical references and index.
ISBN 978-0-7377-5799-6 (hardcover : alk. paper) -- ISBN 978-0-7377-5800-9 (pbk. : alk. paper)
1. Atwood, Margaret, 1939- Handmaid's tale. 2. Women in literature. I. Nelson, David E.
PR9199.3.A8H3664 2012
813'.54--dc23
2011028025

Printed in Mexico
1 2 3 4 5 6 7 15 14 13 12 11

Contents

Chapter 1: Background on Margaret Atwood

Chapter 2: *The Handmaid's Tale* and Women's Issues

Atwood has unfairly—and inconsistently—grouped all conservative Christians into a single authoritarian bogeyman. In railing against this bogeyman, Atwood implicitly defends abortion and pornography as inseparably intermingled rights.

Chapter 3: Contemporary Perspectives on Women's Issues

In April 2006 the US Centers for Disease Control and Prevention released a report recommending that doctors treat all women of childbearing age as being potentially pregnant. While some applauded these recommendations as good and reasonable health care, many saw this as a step toward defining women exclusively in terms of their reproductive roles.

Since the dissolution of the Soviet Union, the Chechen Republic has been politically unstable. As this Sunni Muslim nation becomes increasingly conservative, Chechen women find themselves publicly attacked and humiliated by men who believe these women are not appropriately veiled and modest.

Introduction

Since its publication in 1985, Margaret Atwood's novel *The Handmaid's Tale* has taken on enormous cultural prominence. It is now almost invariably invoked in news items dealing with reproductive rights, religion-driven conservative politics, or the wearing of veils (especially the *hijab* headscarves or *burqa* robes worn by some Muslim women—despite the fact that Muslims are entirely absent from Atwood's novel). Nonetheless, it almost defies credulity that a dystopian sci-fi novel written by a Canadian poet largely unknown outside her country would so quickly earn a perennial position on recommended-reading lists throughout the English-speaking world.

The Handmaid's Tale shot up the *New York Times* bestseller list three times (at its initial publication in 1985, again when the paperback was released in 1987, and once more when the 1990 film version hit theaters). In addition to the 1990 film, *The Handmaid's Tale* has been adapted as radio drama, stage play, and opera. The original book is consistently numbered among the most influential novels of the twentieth century. It is, for instance, number 36 on *Library Journal*'s list of the 150 most influential works of twentieth-century fiction and number 53 on Modern Library's 100 Best Novels list. *The Handmaid's Tale* is also among the most frequently banned books in the United States. It was number 37 on the American Library Association's Top 100 Banned/Challenged Books for the 1990s and number 88 for the first decade of the twenty-first century.

But *The Handmaid's Tale*'s impact was far from assured at its release. While generally positive, many early reviews were mixed; almost all invoked established dystopian novels (especially George Orwell's *1984* and Aldous Huxley's *Brave New World*), implying that Atwood's novel was a somewhat derivative "dystopia for girls." Paul Gray wrote in *Time* magazine (February 10, 1986) that "as a cautionary tale, Atwood's novel lacks the direct, chilling plausibility of *1984* and *Brave New World*. It warns against too much: heedless sex, excessive morality, chemical and nuclear pollution. All of these may be worthwhile targets, but such a future seems more complicated than dramatic." Even established feminists such as Barbara Ehrenreich were not entirely glowing in their assessment. Ehrenreich wrote in the *New Republic* (March 17, 1986) that "Margaret Atwood's new novel is being greeted as the long-awaited feminist dystopia, and I am afraid that for some time it will be viewed as a test of the imaginative power of feminist paranoia. Is Atwood's brave new world really so bad? Is it as ingeniously awful as *1984*? And, by implication, are the fears—or for that matter, the concerns—of feminism worth taking all that seriously?"

Additionally, although the book easily fits into the science fiction category—as do *1984*, *Brave New World*, *Fahrenheit 451*, *A Clockwork Orange*, and the full canon of modern dystopias to which it draws comparison—Atwood has famously and consistently argued that she is no science fiction author and her books are not science fiction novels. This, despite the fact that her four most prominent novels deal in alien life forms, genetic engineering, environmental collapse, and prognosticating the cultural future, and she has won or been nominated for fantasy and sci-fi's most important awards. Although this combative attitude toward science fiction has alienated a devoted community of readers that would have otherwise embraced Atwood's work and ensured her commercial success, the move was savvy. By escaping the genre-fiction label, Atwood brought her work to a much wider audience, to be taken seriously by readers and critics who might otherwise reject science fiction. Atwood subsequently earned worldwide respect; in 2000 she won the Man Booker Prize for Fiction, a prestigious international literary award that has never gone to a "sci-fi writer."

That said, Atwood is no stranger to science and technology. The daughter of a nutritionist and an entomologist, Atwood spent her youth tramping through the Quebec forests surrounding her father's research station. Her brother went on to become a neurophysiologist, while Atwood studied literary theory at the University of Toronto and Harvard. Although she is primarily known as a poet and novelist, she has written and spoken extensively on environmental and energy issues. In 2006 Atwood and her son invented LongPen, a pantographic robotic arm that allows a person to place a legally binding signature on a document from anywhere in the world (provided both the signer and the robot have Internet access). According to Canadian and US law, the resulting signature is just as valid as if it were signed in person.

These contradictions epitomize how it is that Atwood managed to write a novel that is at once political and popular, able to absorb both literary critics and bored kids at the back of class. *The Handmaid's Tale* is born out of the sorts of self-contradictions that do not just populate but define modern life in North America: It is a novel written in the lyric style of a poem; it is a sci-fi horror story grounded in literary fiction's attention to the mundane minutiae of the day-to-day. Like her LongPen, *The Handmaid's Tale* lets readers reach out through space and time to be someplace that they are not, only to discover that they have been there all along.

The following selections examine Margaret Atwood's life, explore from various angles how Atwood addresses women's issues in *The Handmaid's Tale*, and consider ongoing issues facing women in the twenty-first century.

Chronology

1939

Margaret Atwood is born on November 18 in Ottawa, Ontario, Canada, the second of three children, to Margaret Dorothy Killam (a nutritionist), and Carl Edmund Atwood (an entomologist).

1945

Atwood, at age six, begins to write her first novel (soon abandoned).

1946

Atwood's family moves to Toronto.

1952

Atwood begins regularly attending school in the eighth grade.

1955

At age sixteen, Atwood decides to write professionally as a career.

1957–1961

Atwood attends the University of Toronto, earning a bachelor of arts (with honors) in English.

1961

Atwood self-publishes her first chapbook of poetry, *Double Persephone*, which is awarded the E.J. Pratt Medal by the University of Toronto. The same year, Atwood wins the Woodrow Wilson Fellowship to attend Radcliffe College at Harvard University.

1962

Atwood earns her MA from Radcliffe and begins doctoral studies at Harvard.

1963

Atwood returns to Toronto and briefly works for a marketing firm.

1964

Atwood's second poetry collection, *The Circle Game*, is published.

1964–65

Atwood is a lecturer in English at the University of British Columbia.

1966

The Circle Game wins the 1966 Governor General's Award.

1967

Atwood marries Jim Polk.

1967–1968

Atwood teaches at Sir George Williams University in Montreal.

1969

Atwood publishes her first novel, *The Edible Woman*.

1969–1970

Atwood teaches at the University of Alberta.

1971–1972

Atwood is an assistant professor at York University in Toronto.

1972

Atwood publishes her first book of essays, *Survival: A Thematic Guide to Canadian Literature*.

Polk and Atwood separate. (They later divorce.)

Atwood meets her current life partner, novelist Graeme Gibson.

1976

Atwood gives birth to their daughter, Eleanor Jess Atwood Gibson.

1977

Atwood publishes her first collection of short fiction, *Dancing Girls,* which wins the St. Lawrence Award for Fiction and the Periodical Distributors of Canada Award for Short Fiction.

1978

Atwood publishes her first children's book, *Up in the Tree.*

1985

Atwood is MFA honorary chair at the University of Alabama in Tuscaloosa.

The Handmaid's Tale is published.

1986

The Handmaid's Tale is nominated for the Nebula Award.

1987

The Handmaid's Tale is nominated for the Prometheus Award.

The Handmaid's Tale wins the first Arthur C. Clarke Award.

1990

The Handmaid's Tale is adapted to film, directed by Volker Schlöndorff with a screenplay by Harold Pinter.

2000

Poul Ruders's operatic adaptation of *The Handmaid's Tale* premieres in Copenhagen.

The Blind Assassin is published and wins the 2000 Booker Prize.

2003

Atwood publishes *Oryx and Crake*—a speculative novel similar to *The Handmaid's Tale* in its tone and concerns.

2009

Atwood publishes *The Year of the Flood* (which continues along the same lines as *Oryx and Crake*).

Social Issues
in Literature

Background on
Margaret Atwood

The Life of Margaret Atwood

Lee Briscoe Thompson

Lee Briscoe Thompson is emerita professor of English at the University of Vermont and has researched and written extensively about Margaret Atwood and other twentieth-century Canadian writers.

In the following viewpoint, Thompson offers details about Margaret Atwood's upbringing, education, social activism, and writing. Throughout her career Atwood has strenuously resisted being labeled a "genre" author—and rightfully so, as the great bulk of her poetry and prose takes place in recognizably contemporary settings populated with realistic, modern characters. Thompson argues that Atwood's international influence—in the classroom, with critics, and among average readers—has been the consequence of her science fiction and fantasy novels, particularly The Handmaid's Tale. *In the years since this viewpoint was published, Atwood has published two more influential science fiction novels,* Oryx and Crake *(2003) and* The Year of the Flood *(2009).*

Margaret Atwood is arguably the most prominent contemporary Canadian writer. Best known for her novels, Atwood is also admired for her accomplishments as a poet, critic, essayist, and short-story writer, and she has contributed as well to children's fiction, Canadian history, and the editing of volumes ranging from prestigious anthologies to a literary cookbook. The quantity of her output since publishing her first book in 1961 has been impressive, with more than forty books published so far [as of 2001], as well as book reviews and occasional writing of all sorts. In addition, she has worked in other media, including motion pictures, television, theater, cartoons, librettos, and visual art.

Atwood's Education and Writing

Margaret Eleanor Atwood was born on 18 November 1939 in Ottawa, Ontario [Canada] to Margaret Dorothy (Killam) and Carl Edmund Atwood; she was the second of three children. Until her teens Atwood and her family spent much of each year in the bush country of Quebec and Ontario, where her entomologist [insect researcher] father conducted his research, returning to Toronto for the school year. She began to write seriously at the age of sixteen. She attended Victoria College at the University of Toronto from 1957 to 1961, receiving a B.A. with honors in English. She then completed a master's degree in English at Radcliffe College, Harvard University in 1962, and later returned to begin her doctoral studies, which she never completed. Her employment has included a stint as a market researcher in Toronto and teaching positions or writer-in-residence positions at the University of British Columbia, Sir George Williams University (now Concordia University) in Montreal, the University of Alberta, York University in Toronto, the University of Toronto, the University of Alabama, and Macquarie University in Australia. She married James Polk, an American she met at Harvard, on 9 June 1967 in Boston, but they separated in the summer of 1972 and divorced in 1977. Since 1972 her companion has been novelist Graeme Gibson, with whom she has one child, Eleanor Jess, born on 17 May 1976.

Atwood's books, many of them translated into a variety of languages, are frequent selections for high school and university syllabi, and she and her writing have been the subjects of interviews, scholarly and popular articles, reviews, and graduate theses around the world. Further, her involvement with the Writers' Union of Canada and the anglophone [English-speaking] Canadian division of PEN International (in both cases culminating in her service as president), in addition to her roles as a member of the Canadian Civil Liberties Union and the editorial board of the influential Toronto-based House of Anansi Press, and as an outspoken critic of Canadian foreign policy in matters of trade and culture, has also contributed for making her a voice of considerable importance in her native land.

The vast majority of Atwood's fictions have situated themselves firmly in the present—a highly detailed, socially recognizable, North American present day, the second half of the twentieth century—or in the historical past, a painstakingly re-created nineteenth-century Canada, usually in some stage of the Victorian era. Readers of her fiction tend to associate her with realism rather than science fiction, with telling commentary on the ways things were and are rather than the ways they might be. Her most widely known novel, however, *The Handmaid's Tale* (1985), is an obvious and striking exception; it has been described by David Ketterer in the July 1989 issue of *Science-Fiction Studies* as "the best and most successful SF novel written by a Canadian," and it won the first Arthur C. Clarke Award in 1987 for the best science-fiction novel published in a United Kingdom edition the previous year (having also won the Governor-General's Literary Award, the premier Canadian literary award, in 1985). A handful of short stories, the occasional poem, and her later novel *The Blind Assassin* (2000) supplement *The Handmaid's Tale* in demonstrating Atwood's occasional interest in fabulations of future times and in the fantastic.

Speculative, Not Science, Fiction

Atwood herself considers technological gadgetry indispensable to her definition of science fiction, and therefore dismisses the classification of her own work as science fiction because it lacks futuristic hardware. She is more comfortable with the term speculative fiction, which allows the sort of technological regression featured in all of her futuristic works. The term social science fiction also seems applicable to her work, in its pushing of familiar social structures into new configurations, usually dire ones.

Just as Atwood is seen more as a realist than as a science-fiction writer, so too she is not particularly widely viewed as a writer of fantastic fiction. Yet, in her poetry the blurring of the line between the imaginary and the tangible is frequent and often escalates to the point that the "real" is intimated to be an illusion, the unseen more potent and authentic than the seen. (Her poem "Daphne and Laura and So Forth," from her 1995 collection *Morning in the Burned House,* was included in Ellen Datlow and Terri Windling's ninth annual *Year's Best Fantasy and Horror* in 1996.) In her fiction, too, there are many surreal scenes, and characters sometimes move in and out of complex fantasy worlds and lives, parallel universes just a membrane apart. Atwood's inclination to the supernatural arises from her fairytale obsessions and the backwoods animism of her childhood, later compounded by her adult readings of Victorian fantasy and Canadian nature fiction. But ultimately, the reader is almost always presented with confirmations of the ascendancy of consensual reality.

The first of Atwood's occasional stories to speculate on the future or utilize the fantastic is "When It Happens," from her 1977 collection, *Dancing Girls and Other Stories*; it had previously been published in the Canadian women's magazine *Chatelaine* in 1975 and has since been anthologized in the *Penguin Book of Modern Fantasy by Women* (1995). It anticipated *The Handmaid's Tale* in its near-future, familiar setting, in its detailed attention to the gradualness of societal breakdown and yet the rapidity of its impact, and in the paradoxical combination of fearful passivity and resourcefulness with which the protagonist faces change. Mrs. Burridge moves back and forth among her present (the reader's potential near future), her near future (as this present begins to collapse), and her slightly further future (as she travels and encounters her first enemies). While virtually all of the events in the story are clearly expressed as Mrs. Burridge's worried speculations, their foundation is a social upheaval of the near future that has already begun for her (as confirmed by the new need to supplement food stocks by relearning the old art of canning). Further, disastrous developments are so fully realized, both in their vivid descriptions and in the skillful manipulation of verb tenses, that they achieve a reality and certainty of their own; as the title emphasizes, it is not a matter of "if" it happens, but "when."

"Simmering," from the 1983 collection *Murder in the Dark: Short Fictions and Prose Poems*, plays with a future marked by gender role reversal, in an entirely familiar context of barbeques, briefcases, cocktail parties, and kitchen utensils. The story, anticipating Offred's tale-telling in *The Handmaid's Tale*, is a covert narration by a woman who has been officially silenced, who dreams a decidedly female and inclusive dream (one involving both Eden and apples) of freedom, and who seeks to preserve this story by word of mouth and/or manuscript. For once with Atwood, this future is a distant one, many centuries from the present. The tyranny of gender expectations continues, but now men's way of having the upper hand is to be the guardians and repositories of cooking; and since men now do it, the baking of bread has become a profound and sacred rite. The story has considerable fun with all aspects of this rewriting of male dominance, including the transference of their stereotypical preoccupations to applications in what was once the undervalued domestic domain of females and to the sexualization of objects (such as turkey basters and carving knives) that had no such cachet in the hands of women. This future society has finally gotten women out of the kitchen, but in this recast universe that means they are still excluded from the sites of power.

Atwood Attains Worldwide Prominence

The Handmaid's Tale, published in 1985, was on *The New York Times* Best Sellers list for fifteen weeks at first release, and again for eight weeks when released as a paperback in 1987,

Margaret Atwood, author of The Handmaid's Tale, *on August 19, 2009.* © The Canadian Press/Darren Calabrese/AP Images.

with a further four weeks in 1990 after the movie version appeared. It was a crucial crossover book for Atwood. Before that, she had been the darling of Canadian poetry lovers, fans of contemporary fiction, and women's studies specialists. But with *The Handmaid's Tale* Atwood acquired a huge popular readership and also attracted the attention of scholars in many fields outside literature. The novel began appearing in courses and articles on political science, history, sociology, philosophy, theology, environmental studies, and human biology. A large component of its initial appeal had to do with the compelling—to many readers, terrifying—vision it offered of a society of the near future, an exaggeration for (a little) better and for (the most part) worse of the reader's own, recognizable contemporary scene.

The Handmaid's Tale envisions a white, right-wing, theocratic coup having taken place in the northeast United States of the early twenty-first century. An autocratic elite, alarmed by a precipitous decline in Caucasian birth rates and by the degeneration of a "traditional" American society, has master-minded the murder of the president and a massacre in Congress, then played on public fear, ignorance, and restricted access to information and money to suspend all civil rights. A frightened, confused citizenry has hunkered down to ride out the crisis, and most have submitted meekly to the rapid imposition of many restrictions and a rigid codification of status and role in the new, dystopian state of Gilead.

Most dramatically and visibly, women are stripped of jobs and financial independence and pressed into one of eight color-coded categories: Wives of the elite (blue), young Daughters of the elite (white), Widows (black), Aunts (khaki), Handmaids (red), Marthas (dull green), Econowives (red/blue/green stripes), and Unwomen (grey). Jezebels, an unofficial group of women coerced into prostitution, are assigned a ragbag of frazzled, flashy outfits once associated with eroticism. Although virtually powerless, the group at the center of this structure is the Handmaids, fertile women forcibly recruited to try to bear children for the older, all too often sterile Commanders. All other positions, male and female, in the society revolve around the core mission of reproduction, and the myriad aspects of repression considered necessary to enforce compliance and rebuild the white population (people of color having been "relocated").

Joining the Ranks of Classic Dystopias

The Handmaid's Tale purports to be the transcript of one Handmaid's description of her life in the early days of the Gilead regime, in the transition generation caught between memories of life in "the time before" (the late twentieth century) and the powerful indoctrination of Gilead. Offred's tale is followed by another transcript, from a convention two hundred years later, in which academics meet to discuss the by-then defunct Gilead from the perspective of the year 2195. One arresting (and by no means reassuring) characteristic of

Gilead and of the world of 2195 is that they seem so unfuturistic, in the sense that the artifacts, attitudes, customs, idiom, and actions seem quite familiar and largely unchanged from those of contemporary society. True, there is a long list of compu-items in use in Gilead (such as Compubite, Compudoc, and Compubank), but society in 1985 had already progressed to nearly that degree, and Atwood's vision of a future cashless society seems not far off. However, Gilead has regressed considerably in the realm of technology, and indeed has done so as a matter of policy, for it blames science for having contributed to the mess that necessitated a coup (artificial insemination and birth control, toxic chemicals and wastes, nuclear accidents, and so on). In consequence, women in Gilead give birth without anesthetics or surgical assistance; written language has shrunk to pictograms for all but the elite and their enforcers, the Aunts; the sexes are once again segregated and chaperoned, the women often veiled and restricted to lives without mechanical or even cosmetic aids; and televisions and other machines have only the most curtailed place in daily life. Although some phrases from the time before have lost currency there is no Orwellian Newspeak.

Nor, in the North America of 2195 when the scholarly symposium takes place in Nunavit to study Gilead, does much appear to have changed from the reader's time. There is a little window dressing in the elevation of ethnic and female academics, but a condescending keynote speaker from England makes clear that colonialism and sexism are still firmly in place. Atwood's interest in the future appears most importantly to have to do with affirming the adage that "the more things change, the more they stay the same," and with issuing a warning that humans are not really that far from nightmarish extensions of the current world. By minimizing the number of differences between her two futures (Gilead and Nunavit) and the present, and by emphasizing that everything in Gilead has historical precedent, Atwood produces a speculative fiction that holds readers close to home and intensifies their nervousness that such things could happen. Good utopian and dystopian fiction depends on the reader's consciousness of the connection between reality and fictional future, if the vision is to have power and point. *The Handmaid's Tale* makes that connection and shows how relevant her cautionary tale is.

Like many other dystopian narratives, *The Handmaid's Tale* conjures up a future based on an extreme extrapolation of contemporary conditions. The novel furnishes standard dystopian features: lack of freedom, relentless surveillance, imposed routine, an abortive escape attempt, and an underground resistance. It has often been compared and contrasted with such dystopian classics as Aldous Huxley's *Brave New World* (1932), George Orwell's *Nineteen Eighty-Four* (1949). Evgenii Zamiatin's *We* (1924), Ray Bradbury's *Fahrenheit 451* (1953), and Anthony Burgess's *A Clockwork Orange* (1962), and the majority of assessments have ranked Atwood's novel on a par with and sometimes even superior to those classics.

Critics Respond to *The Handmaid's Tale*

The Handmaid's Tale has been extensively discussed by literary scholars. Some critics have argued that it failed as a dystopia, suggesting that the world of Gilead is utterly improbable and underdeveloped, and complaining that Atwood had sacrificed serious social criticism to romance rhetoric, mere entertainment, and/or costume Gothicism. Some felt that *The Handmaid's Tale* showed a failure of futuristic imagination, evinced in the fact that it modified in the invented future so little of the linguistic, environmental, philosophical, and social framework of the present. Yet the majority of critics have argued that *The Handmaid's Tale* presents an effective warning against absolutist or despotic systems, using a near-future projection to show the relationship between general power structures or ideologies and the individual. Many critics took the position that Atwood had transformed the genre and produced a feminist dystopia. [David] Ketterer speculated that the difference lay in the fact that Atwood's dystopia moves circularly, rather than linearly as was "traditional," which consequentially blunted the satire and anger with the implication that incarnations of Gilead will keep recurring. He then argued that *The Handmaid's Tale* was successful precisely because of this innovative indirection and understatement, features vilified by impatient critics expecting a more crisply efficient brand of totalitarianism than that of Gilead, a more monstrous oppressor than Commander Fred, and a less tricksterish narrator than Offred. Critics making the case of *The Handmaid's Tale* as a feminist dystopia often cited as feminist deviations from the male dystopian model the very "subversive" strategies criticized elsewhere as flaws: irrepressible humor, creativity, self-assertion, open-endedness, wordplay, Offred's fluid identity, irony, narrative evasions (including contradictory but equally valorized plot-lines), overthrow of archetypes (such as light for knowledge and darkness for ignorance, disrupted by the Night chapters), and sheer survival.

For some readers the strongest alarm sounded by this novel has been environmental, a concern that links it to many other Atwood pieces. Like many conjurers of the future, Atwood fears for the planet, and her childhood experiences as the daughter of a cheerfully pessimistic entomologist, spending more than half of each year in the wilds of the Canadian Shield, have given her the ecological documentation to support those fears. In her novel the Gileadeans appear to have pulled back from the environmental abyss in time, but they now err in their extreme tampering with human nature. And, in the appended Historical Notes the dispassionate scholarly observers of Gilead two centuries later are shown to have learned little from Offred's tale. Atwood everywhere asserts humankind's capacity to destroy its surroundings and its species.

The Handmaid's Tale is by far Atwood's most influential and best-known contribution to Canadian science fiction, though she has continued to explore speculative or fantastic elements. . . .

Although only a small portion of Atwood's work can be truly classified as science fiction, *The Handmaid's Tale* and the scattering of other speculative work that she has published so far have helped to make readers aware of Canadian science fiction. Certainly, science-fiction conventions have influenced her work and provided her with another means of exploring gender politics and environmental issues, which are the two paramount concerns that inform Atwood's futurist and fantasy fiction.

The Impact of
Feminism, Postcolonialism,
and Utopianism
on Atwood's Writing

Margaret Atwood, as told to Danita J. Dodson

Danita J. Dodson is an educator who has extensively researched the literature of utopia and dystopia, including Atwood's The Handmaid's Tale.

The following viewpoint, drawn from Danita J. Dodson's 1994 interview with Margaret Atwood, delves into Atwood's background—her intellectual interests as well as her formal academic work at Harvard—to demonstrate how literacy is central to both Atwood's writing and her political beliefs. Since Canadian-born Atwood did her undergraduate work at the University of Toronto, she came to both Harvard and American literature (which she studied exhaustively, from the colonial period forward) without preconceived notions. Dodson also explores the role that feminism, postcolonialism, and utopianism have played in Atwood's writing, especially in The Handmaid's Tale.

The following interview, conducted in May 1994, is Atwood's commentary on the intertwined topics of feminism, postcolonialism, and utopianism. Basing her discussion loosely around the dystopian novel *The Handmaid's Tale*, she reveals a knowledge of colonial literature, an understanding of women's roles in recording the frontier experience, and a sensitivity to the continuum of oppression around the globe. She weaves together a discussion of historical situations with observations about contemporary ones. Thus, from an initial fo-

Danita J. Dodson, "An Interview with Margaret Atwood," *Critique: Studies in Contemporary Fiction*, 1997, Vol. 38:2 p. 96. Copyright © 1997, Taylor and Francis Books, Ltd. Reproduced by permission.

cus on a specific novel and a particular genre the interview moves toward a more global and political dialogue about equality and the structures of power.

A US Academic Background

Danita J. Dodson: I wish to speak with you today about the historical implications of The Handmaid's Tale. *I am specifically concerned with your quite disturbing portrayal of the colonialist politics of the regime of Gilead. How has your association with the colonial history of the United States influenced your illustration of an American continuum of imperialist ventures?*

Margaret Atwood: Okay, let's do a little background here. Number one: two bunches of my ancestors were dealing with Puritans. Number two: I did go to Harvard, where the novel is essentially set. And while there—you know this because you're a Ph.D. student—I had to write exams in five different areas of literature in English, four of them being English literature from England and one of them being American literature. I had gone through the Honor's English program at the University of Toronto, when there still was such a thing, but it went from Anglo-Saxon to T.S. Eliot basically, and did not do much American literature. So I had to study American literature at Harvard, and not just American literature meaning [Ernest] Hemingway and [William] Faulkner, but starting in the seventeenth century. So I studied with Perry Miller, and as you probably know, he was the man who more or less resurrected the study of seventeenth-century Puritans in America. So that's part of that kind of background. And it was, of course, very interesting to be in a place with which I had ancestral connections. It was evident to me, as it was evident to anybody who has ever studied it, that the fairy tale version that kids used to get in school—the Puritans came to America to establish a democracy—was quite wrong. They were not interested in democracy. In fact, it wasn't even a notion at that time. They were interested in a theocracy, their rules. And among the things they did, in addition to participating in witchcraft persecutions, they persecuted basically anybody who didn't agree with them religiously. So Quakers were fair game, and you probably know of the expulsion of Anne Hutchinson. And, as you probably also know, the seventeenth century was a particularly bad century for misogyny. There were some gains for women coming from the Protestant end of things—they were encouraged to read, so they could read the Bible. One of the things that the Protestant Reformation did was to essentially remove the feminine elements in Roman Catholicism. It removed, demoted, the Virgin Mary and it got rid of the saints (a number of the saints had been female). But Protestantism, because it emphasized a return to the Word, did away with images as much as it could. It really emphasized the parts of the Bible that were very male centered. There are all kinds of ways of reading the Bible, and one way, which is returning, is to look at the kinds of metaphors used, and certainly some of the kinds of metaphors that Christ uses in the New Testament are female. But that isn't what they [Puritans] were interested in at all. It was interesting to me, when I was studying American literature at that time, which was the early 60s—I did the whole thing, the official canon— there were only two women honored [poets Anne Bradstreet and Emily Dickinson]. . . .

Something I've noted, and this ties in with your preparation for your Ph.D., is that imperialism and colonialism entail journey and movement. And I've read of your interest in quest stories.

US vs. Canadian Colonial Female Writers

There are literary quests. What you are talking about is immigration stories, and I've certainly written about that; in fact, I have a book called *The Journals of Susanna Moody*, which is based on an English woman's immigration to Canada, what happened to her there in the nineteenth century. One difference between Canada and the States is that some of the earliest literature in Canada, in both French and English, is by women, so that when you study Canadian literature you can't just ignore them. You have to deal with them. Some of the earliest things written down in the northern North American continent were written by French nuns moving over to Quebec. And then there was a huge wave of English-speaking immigration, or I should say, British Isles immigration, in the late eighteenth and nineteenth centuries due to three factors: (1) Scottish clearances, which means there are now as many Gaelic speakers in Nova Scotia as there are in Scotland, (2) the Irish potato famine, (3) the end of the Napoleonic Wars, which threw a lot of career military, traditionally younger sons, out of work. And the British government, which was trying to get a lot of English speakers into Canada, offered free land. But the upshot of that was—say that New England was settled in the seventeenth century by the Puritans who did not encourage women—English Canada was settled in the eighteenth and nineteenth centuries, and the number of those women who came were not only already literate, they were already practicing writers. So the early literary periods of both countries look somewhat different.

Yes. Questing, I have heard you say, in women's literature has been internalized, but those early stories, by Canadian women were actually about physical mobility.

Yes, yes. And they weren't fiction; they were accounts. Just as the early American literature is accounts and sermons in the seventeenth century, so you'll get physical descriptions of where they were and what they were doing, and then you'll get religious interpretations of that, and you'll get sermons, and you'll get individual journals, but you will not get novels. Well, the novel didn't really come into its own until the nineteenth century anyway, so why would you expect novels? But you would not get, for instance, plays; they didn't allow plays anyway. So mostly when people arrived in Canada, their first response was not to write a novel about it; their first response was to write an account, and these accounts were usually written for the people in the country that they had come from. In fact, Susanna Moody's book *Roughing in the Bush* was essentially a book directed to English persons of the middle class, telling them not to do it: "This is too hard for you. Don't do it. Stay where you are."

Was there any mention of destroying the wilderness, or sadness?

Oh, they didn't think of it as destroying it; they thought of it as cultivating it. But it was a huge period where this whole area was covered by enormous trees, and you cannot have a farm with wheat on it with enormous trees. So their first idea was to get rid of as many trees as they could, and if you look at pictures of the time you will see log cabins surrounded by stumps, no ornamental plantings. They wanted the trees as far away from the house as they could get them because they were terrified of forest fires. Anyway none of this has much to do with *The Handmaid's Tale*. . . .

The Handmaid's Tale in Dystopia Tradition

The Handmaid's Tale then is an American vision of how a woman has been prohibited from this venture and quest. Right?

It's a dystopia, number one, and, therefore, the literary tradition to which it belongs is that of utopias and dystopias, going all the way back to Plato, the book of Revelation, on up through Sir Thomas More and Jonathan Swift, and then into the nineteenth century with people like William Morris. And utopias and dystopias have a lot of things in common. Although one is depicting ideal society and the other is depicting its opposite, their areas of interest are still very similar. They both are, as it were, blueprints for a society, and they express interest in a lot of the same areas, mainly what do you do about sex? What do you do about the distribution of goods? What do you do about who is in charge? What do you do about punishment? It's interesting to me that in Thomas More's [*Utopia*] the punishment for adultery is enslavement. What do you do about disease? What do you do about . . . essentially all of the problems societies deal with anyway. Except these utopias and dystopias deal with them in imagined forms. And in a dystopia, of course, power is absolute and control of sex is also very stringent. And in utopias power is usually either benevolent or shared, and you often find some version of either free love or pleasurable sex. And why was [Gilead] in the States rather than in Canada? Because Canada is fifty percent Catholic. What you really need to control any society is twenty-five percent of the populace, and if you're trying to set up a theocracy, which is what Gilead is, you wouldn't be able to get that in Canada.

So Gilead is not possible in Canada?

Much less likely. Canada is too diverse. Remember that a third of it is French speaking. So you might postulate a Gilead in, say, a province of Canada, but it would be hard to do in the whole thing.

So borders, labels, divisions are more distinct in Canada than in America?

I think it's harder to get all the lemmings headed for the same cliff.

Offred, is she a questor? Maybe internally? I've heard you mention that . . .

Well, she doesn't like where she is, but neither does Winston Smith [in Orwell's *Nineteen Eighty-Four*]. Dystopias are places in which you don't like where you are; that's what they are by definition.

And one feels a need to move beyond.

Well, dystopias by definition are places in which it is very difficult to move.

But there is the desire.

Margaret Atwood poses for a photograph on February 1, 1978. © Sophie Bassouls/Sygma/ Corbis.

Survival Under Totalitarianism

Well, would you want to be her [Offred]? . . . No. On the other hand, what are her choices? This is the other thing about totalitarianism, which people who live in free societies often find it difficult to understand, choices are extremely limited. There are some. That is, she knows people who belong to an underground; there is an underground. It's very dangerous to belong to it. And that's another thing that young people sometimes don't get; they say, "Oh, why don't they all just go join the underground?" I recommend to them that they get out a German movie called *The White Rose*, which is about a group of German university students who were against the Nazis, organizing and printing pamphlets and stuff; they were all shot. It's the risking your life part that Americans don't usually get because they've seen too many Hollywood movies in which the good guys win. In real life the good guys often don't win.

Could it be that we Americans are not equipped with those survival skills that you attribute to the Canadians?

No, I don't think Canadians have them either.

Really?

No, we [Canadians and Americans] live in rather pampered democracies. Who you really need to talk to about some of this stuff is somebody who went through [Joseph] Stalin, somebody who went through [Adolf] Hitler. Your choices were to get out of the country if you could, keep your mouth shut and go along with everything, or risk your life and join an underground movement, all of which were routinely infiltrated.

Quest implies ability to move beyond borders. Your involvement with Amnesty International represents your own work toward liberating political prisoners.

Well, you make it sound as if I did a lot of work with them, and I have supported them, but I do more work with P.E.N. Writers in Prison.

Could that be something that a prisoner like Offred could be saved by?

It wouldn't be allowed to operate in a dictatorship like Gilead. It could only exist as an underground network. And one of my models for what's happening in the underground movement in Gilead is the Underground Railroad, which was very illegal and undercover.

Oh, could you talk about that a bit? I'm interested in that analogy.

Well, the same people are involved in both [underground movements]. That's why I have the Quakers involved in rescuing women; that's what the Quakers would do under these circumstances because they were involved in the Underground Railroad [during the American Civil War].

Freedom, Equality, and Literacy

You may disagree or agree, but I feel that you present, among many other illustrations of types of oppression throughout the world, a rich portrait of the African American female slave in The Handmaid's Tale. *A critic, in fact, has said that "The closest corollary to the Gileadean system is slavery in the American South, when black women were similarly prized and priced as breeders."*

Absolutely. And the other thing I use from that situation is that black people, in general, were forbidden by law to read.

Or write.

Or write. They were forbidden to be literate. Similarly with women, If you look at world illiteracy rates, by the way, they are way higher amongst women.

Today, even?

Today, oh yes. I'm talking about countries like India and South America. Of the people who can read or write, they are much more likely to be men.

Is it fair to say that maybe your study or recognition of the African American experience then is embedded within the book intentionally?

Oh, certainly. It's absolutely fair to say it. But, you see, it's not just African Americans; it's slavery in general. Or, say, oppression in general. One of the things that oppressors like to deny, and usually do, to the people that they are oppressing is education. And it was the same with the upper classes in England versus the working classes. You don't want the people that you're oppressing to be able to read. It gives them ideas. And similarly with women; they get ideas if they read.

Making this analogy between races of people who are enslaved and women who are enslaved, do you see that there are some similarities between the goals of feminism and what is now called postcolonialism?

Well, they're both concerned with the bringing [of] equality [to] groups that have not been equal. So they're both concerned with the rearranging of previous power structures. Now there're all kinds of ways that that breaks down within those kinds of groups. But if you had to pick out one overriding theme that would probably be it. The other thing that is evident in *The Handmaid's Tale* is apartheid. . . . Gilead sets up national homelands and puts all the black people in them. And it's the same that South Africa did until—until a couple of days ago.[1]

It's strange that you mention that, but I had planned to ask you how you feel about that situation.

Making a Perfect World

We're living in an extraordinary time. When you think that within the past five years, the Wall [dividing Soviet East Berlin from democratic West Berlin] has come down, the Soviet Empire has crumbled, the Palestinians and the Israelis seem about to work something out, and South Africa has given universal suffrage to blacks. And it's just incredible. Ten years ago you never would have thought you would have seen any of these things happening very soon at all. So it's really been amazing when you come to think of it. We've also seen some very bad things. We've seen Rwanda, we've seen Yugoslavia, just to name a couple of things. We're seeing vicious local wars, and that comes with the removal of the Cold War. There're no longer controlling patron powers. So when you take the lid off, everything boils out.

It's probably harder for those people who have been under oppression so long to learn to build a society, a perfect world.

Well, I think it's more like this. I think that a place like Yugoslavia got freedom strained when [Yugoslavian authoritarian president Josip] Tito came in and simply made disparate groups get along. Then that collapses and the disparate groups,

1. Former political prisoner Nelson Mandela was elected president of South Africa on April 27, 1994 (just a couple of days before this interview took place), effectively ending apartheid.

who have not forgotten their differences, are free to buy weapons and shoot each other, which they then proceed to do. The amazing thing about South Africa so far is how diplomatically and skillfully Mandela has been handling it.

I must tell you—and this gets back into the desire for a better world—that your novel, The Handmaid's Tale, *inspired my entire study of the genre of utopian and dystopian fiction.*

Oh, I'm happy.

I read it in 1991 for the first time, and it moved me so that I began to read backwards in the canon, in the genre. And I think it's a unique situation. I read the re-vision of the canon before I read the canon. So as a utopianist myself, tempered by visions of dystopia, I must ask you: what is your view of a perfect world? I know that's a very tough question to answer.

That's a very tough question.

You did write that you agree with [American novelist] Flannery O'Connor that "people without hope do not write novels."

Yes, that's true. Well, I think there's a human paradox, which is that hell is what you often get when you try to impose heaven. The key word is "impose." I don't think that, subject as we are to the laws of chemistry and physics, we are ever going to have "a perfect world"—by that I mean one in which no one ever dies, everybody is happy all the time, nobody ever gets sick, everything always goes well. We can't hope for that. What we can hope for is human cooperation, and this is what is different from the word "impose." So I think that you only can get something better when you don't try to take a kind of cookie cutter and stamp out a limited idea, or one person's idea, or one group's idea of what is convenient.

The New Feudalism

Do you foresee a day when borders will be more clearly marked, or will the postmodern internationalism of world communications and commercialism lead to a loss of nationalism?

We are going back to a kind of feudalism. There are nation states. And think of the international corporations as the barons. The difference is that now we don't need castles. You now have a group of feudal lords who are attached by internet.

Technology is rearranging our lives.

Yes. What usually scares readers is when the women [of Gilead] go to the store and the computers inform them that their credit cards are void. How often does that happen now, when we are told "I'm sorry, but your credit has been overextended?"

It seems a real possibility. So we shouldn't sit complacent with the view that "it can't happen here"?

Who was it that said "Vigilance is the eternal price of freedom"?

I don't know. Who?

I don't know, but it was one of you guys [Americans]. If you really want to worry about the future, you need climatic change. Everything depends upon the earth.

Politics and American Literature

I think that in The Handmaid's Tale *you point to a major necessity of a revision of the women's movement and offer a prophecy of what can happen if central feminisms aren't displaced. The split between Offred and Serena Joy, for example, sadly highlights a difference between women. What is your opinion of how women can bond across economic lines and color bars and nationalities?*

It's a possibility, but we need to understand that women are not homogenous, just as men are not all the same. You can't say woman with a capital W. This is a cookie cutter approach to women, much as in the 19th century. I've always liked variety. Women are never going to agree about everything, for example, about fashion. It's hard for people to cooperate. They have to work at it. You know how Canadians do it? Canadian negotiation is around the table—we don't stop until everybody is in agreement. And that sometimes takes a long time.

Many theorize that today is a period of postfeminism. Do you agree?

No. It's a different phase of feminism. But we're still faced with many of the same questions that women were faced with in the past.

You are without a doubt a very political writer. Do you feel that many writers in the States today, including women, have cut themselves off from politics, feeling that the political is anti-literary?

That's not true. Take a look at [prominent African American novelist and professor] Toni Morrison. The opinion that American writers are not political will be voiced most often in poetic workshops. But anyone who examines society is political. Every human being has a component from which they examine society. To be human is to be aware of your surroundings. To be aware of your surroundings then is to be aware, in [*Animal Farm* author George] Orwell's words, that "All animals are created equal. But some animals are more equal than others." . . .

Social Issues
in Literature

CHAPTER 2

The Handmaid's Tale and Women's Issues

The Handmaid's Tale Addresses Sexism and Ignores Racism

Ben Merriman

Ben Merriman teaches at the University of Chicago in the Department of Sociology, where his research interests include comparative and historical sociology as well as social theory.

In the following viewpoint, Merriman argues that in The Handmaid's Tale, *Atwood has essentially equated many aspects of the inequality experienced by women with the widespread and brutal subjugation of African Americans under slavery. According to Merriman, by glossing over the African American experience of slavery—which Atwood clearly borrows from and recasts in framing Offred's plight—Atwood unintentionally creates a "politically hazardous fantasy" in which white American women have suffered to the same extent as African Americans. Merriman is concerned that such a fantasy might lead readers to incorrectly estimate the continuing importance of race in the United States.*

White privilege is rarely manifested in intentional, positive acts. It is, in Peggy McIntosh's terms, "invisible," "unearned," and "cashed in each day." To be White is to be the norm, universal. This norm functions automatically, and unless the universality of White experience is explicitly questioned or subverted, racial distortions may appear even against the conscious intent of an author.

Ben Merriman, "White-Washing Oppression in Atwood's *The Handmaid's Tale*," *Notes on Contemporary Literature*, January 2009. Copyright © 2009, Notes on Contemporary Literature. Reproduced by permission.

A Politically Hazardous Fantasy

Such distortions appear throughout Margaret Atwood's *The Handmaid's Tale*. Atwood attempts to offer an archetypal account of female exploitation, but the stand-in for this universal experience is Offred, a White, college-educated American. Offred would seem an unlikely victim, but at no point in the text does Atwood acknowledge that sexism in America has, generally, been modulated by forms of race and class oppression, nor does she acknowledge the parallels between her own story and the experience of Black slavery. Because these historically specific oppressions are removed from their broader context, the *Tale* drifts from speculative fiction, which is anchored in reality, into conceptually suspect and politically hazardous fantasy.

Atwood's dystopia is set in the late 20th Century, when a cadre of fundamentalist Christians have overthrown the U.S. government and created the theocratic Republic of Gilead. Due to an unexplained fertility crisis, the government has impressed unmarried women of proven fertility into a state of sexual servitude. Many others work as domestic slaves in an autarkic [self-sufficient and independent], inefficient command economy. Women are forbidden to read or to meet without supervision. The novel thus places particular emphasis on the most persistent forms of female victimization: the sexual exploitation, isolation, and compelled ignorance that accompany severe economic and political powerlessness.

These forms of victimization do not function in a vacuum, and in the United States they have been associated most strongly with the enslavement of African-Americans. Forced procreation arose from widespread slavery associated with plantation agriculture, particularly during the 19th Century, when the Trans-Atlantic slave trade was on the wane and industrialization increased the demand for raw materials. This form of abuse followed a specific vector, from the White slaveholding man to the Black enslaved woman.

Unearned Parallels to Black Slavery

In *The Handmaid's Tale*, victimization does appear to function in a historical and causal vacuum. The Republic of Gilead is an all-White enclave, and Blacks are erased from the novel in a single line, cloaked in Old Testament euphemism:

> 'Resettlement of the Children of Ham is continuing on schedule,' says the reassuring pink face, back on the screen. 'Three thousand have arrived this week in National Homeland One, with another two thousand in transit.'

While the demand for Black slaves had a well-established economic cause, Offred is forced to copulate because of the novel's two ill-supported pretenses: the coup, which is glossed over in less than a paragraph, and the nebulous, unexplained "fertility crisis." These are clearly fantastic rather than speculative devices, and it is only by this inventive leap that Atwood can write a White professional into the position of a Black slave.

The restrictions on reading and assembly in the *Tale* are similarly contrived. Tight controls on literacy have been the norm throughout Christian history, but these controls have not been exclusively gendered. The hegemony of Latin into the 16th Century functioned as a form of class oppression. In the Antebellum South, restrictions on literacy were based on race, not gender, and here Atwood again draws from the precedent of Black slavery without acknowledgement. The novel is understood to be a transcript of a recitation given by Offred on the night of her escape into Canada. In the slave narrative genre, the "orality" of the text owed to the illiteracy of the narrator, or to the fact that the narrative was recited for a gathered crowd. Offred, a former librarian, is highly literate, and she is speaking to a tape recorder. This orality has the putative function of letting Offred's fate remain unknown to the reader. However, its deeper function is precisely the opposite.

Leaving Offred in suspension, without access to paper, allows Atwood to maintain the increasingly dubious parallels to the experience of slavery.

The Perniciousness of White Privilege

Atwood's intentions for writing *The Handmaid's Tale* are noble, and most readers find it smooth and convincing. It is thus an object lesson in the pernicious character of White Privilege—a well-written, imaginative, and humane novel can nonetheless hide the link between racism and sexism. In fact, Atwood's exercise of racial privilege is more problematic because of her talent. She deftly parodies the clumsy language of racial propaganda and offers a convincing portrait of the placid, banal evil of the religious extremist. The intersection between race and sex is itself hidden in plain sight, in the improbable but extremely sympathetic Offred, and only a cad would greet her with suspicion.

The Handmaid's Tale Is a Defense of Abortion and Pornography

Anne Barbeau Gardiner

Anne Barbeau Gardiner is professor emeritus of English at John Jay College and a contributing editor to the New Oxford Review, *an orthodox Catholic magazine that explores issues of faith and culture. She is a frequent book reviewer and critic and the author of* Ancient Faith and Modern Freedom in John Dryden's "The Hind and the Panther."

In the following viewpoint, Gardiner argues that The Handmaid's Tale *is essentially a confused feminist erotic-horror story that implicitly defends both abortion and pornography, treating them as inseparable rights. The author notes that Atwood has unfairly—and inconsistently—folded the entire spectrum of conservative Christianity into a monstrous authoritarian bogeyman that has never existed and likely could never exist.*

The culture of death, being a parody of the culture of life, is also a seamless garment. For over a century now there has been an interrelated defense of abortion and pornography. The Comstock Act of 1873 made the link explicit between obscenity and abortion when it banned the mailing not only of every obscene writing or picture but also of anything meant for "preventing conception or producing abortion." It is no accident that Planned Parenthood, now the biggest provider of abortion in the U.S., boasts of having played a major role in overturning both the Comstock Act of 1873 and the Commu-

Anne Barbeau Gardiner, "The Interrelated Defense of Abortion and Pornography in Margaret Atwood's *The Handmaid's Tale*," *Life and Learning XIII: UFL Life and Learning*, 2003, Vol. 13, pp. 89–98. Copyright © 2003, University for Life Faculty. Reproduced by permission.

nications Decency Act of 1996, thus opening the floodgates to pornography in the U.S. mails and on the Internet.

Abortion and Birth Control Parallel

A good example of an interrelated defense of abortion and pornography in literature can be found in the novel *The Handmaid's Tale* by Canadian author Margaret Atwood. . . .

Let us see what Atwood says explicitly about abortion in her novel. In the last part of her book, she imagines a professor of the late twenty-second century giving a paper about the causes of the white population's decline and extinction in the U.S. He declares that only "some of the failure to reproduce" could be attributed to "birth control of various kinds, including abortion." Atwood here makes her learned speaker define abortion as a form of *birth control*. With a flourish, she makes twenty million babies aborted in the U.S. from 1973 to 1986 disappear into thin air, their absence equated with their never having existed. Atwood's professor then spells out the reason for the population decline: environmental poisons from "nuclear-plant accidents," "leakages from chemical and biological warfare stockpiles," "toxic waste," insecticides and herbicides. Atwood wants to displace the blame for the absence of children from the sex and abortion industries to the Pentagon and big business. Since Atwood calls abortion "birth control," it is noteworthy that Moira, the heroine of her novel, worked in the publishing division of a women's collective before the revolution, putting out "books on birth control." In other words, she was a propagandist for abortion.

Atwood depicts pro-life Christians as becoming violent once they establish their theocracy: they proclaim all doctors who ever committed abortions "war criminals" retroactively guilty of "atrocities" against humanity. They sift through the few hospital records that survive or use informants to ferret out the former abortionists and to execute them publicly. When the narrator first approaches the Wall of Harvard yard in Cambridge, Mass., there are six dead doctors and scientists in white coats hanging on hooks for their crimes of abortion: "Each has a placard hung around his neck to show why he has been executed, a drawing of a human fetus."

Demonizing the Entire Christian Right

Atwood leaves it vague just who these tyrannical Christians are, for she shows them persecuting only some Catholics, Jews, Baptists, and Presbyterians, but all Quakers, blacks, and homosexuals. In her *Ms.* [magazine] interview, Atwood calls attention to the "civil war" that in her *Tale* is "led" by Southern Baptists. One reviewer finds it odd that Southern Baptists should lead a counter-revolution against a fundamentalist theocracy, and he calls this only one of her "ignorant" misrepresentations of the American Christian Right. In fact, it is not ignorance, but an attempt to lull the expected opposition.

To make sure that the reader does not attribute any humane motive to Christians for their opposition to abortion, Atwood depicts them as quietly committing infanticide on a vast scale. The narrator explains that while abortion is outlawed in the theocracy, defective newborns disappear without a trace: "You can't have them taken out; whatever it is must be carried to term." But if they have "a pinhead or a snout like a dog's, or two bodies, or a hole in its heart or no arms, or webbed hands and feet," they are "declared Unbabies" and "put somewhere, quickly, away." Also, fetuses are valued only if they are not defective. The narrator describes a procession of lower-class women in black mourning a miscarriage, the mother carrying a small jar with a fetus only two or three months old, "too young to tell whether or not it was an Unbaby." The point is that if the fetus were imperfect, it would be thrown away, not given a funeral. In this way, Atwood projects the culture of death's utilitarian view of babies, born and unborn, onto the culture of life, showing Christians as hypocrites who use the Bible to persecute women and exploit them for purposes of eugenics.

To underline the inhumanity of right-to-lifers, the narrator also recalls that they had the name "*bleeders*" before the revolution because they used to carry signs saying, "*Let them bleed.*" In short, she imputes such a hatred of women to Christian conservatives that she imagines them carrying signs that tell women to go bleed to death in illegal abortions. This is just one example of how she uses a wide brush to tar the entire Christian Right in this story.

Abortion Linked to Pornography

Let's now examine how the defense of pornography is closely interrelated with that of abortion in Atwood's *Tale*. The narrator remembers that her mother joined in many marches before the revolution: "[I]t was during the time of the porn riots, or was it the abortion riots, they were close together. There were a lot of bombings then: clinics, video stores; it was hard to keep track." The implication here is that great numbers of Christians were bombing both abortion clinics and porn shops at once—a malicious fantasy, since violence has always been very rare on the Christian side. At the time, the narrator's mother was a feminist who actively defended abortion, yet she marched with Christians against pornography. One reviewer noted that there had indeed been an alliance of feminists and fundamentalists to fight porn in the early 1980s, and another explained that Atwood herself had been against porn earlier on.

When the narrator is undergoing training as a "handmaid," she watches a documentary in which her mother marches with a group bearing such banners as: "Freedom to choose. Every baby a wanted baby. Recapture our bodies." Also, as she grew up, the narrator would often hear her mother say, "You were a wanted child, all right," the phrase "wanted child" being a mantra of the abortion-rights party. Clearly, her mother was a militant defender of abortion. Yet Atwood portrays this older feminist as very misguided for joining an "ecstatic" group of women who burned porn in a public space. The narrator was only a child then, but she recalls her mother giving her a magazine to throw on the flames. She looked at the cover and saw that it had "a pretty woman on it, with no clothes on, hanging from the ceiling by a chain wound around her hand." She adds, the picture "didn't frighten me. I thought she was swinging, like Tarzan from a vine." But when she threw the magazine on the fire, something sinister happened: "flakes of paper came loose . . . parts of women's bodies turning to black ash, in the air, before my eyes." This imagery suggests that looking at porn is harmless, even for a child, but burning it is murderous: it sends out "parts of women's bodies" into the air as "black ash." Thus, Atwood links the burning of porn to the burning of women in gas ovens, one of her many allusions to the Third Reich. Several reviewers noted these allusions, one of them calling the narrator of the *Tale* "a latter-day Anne Frank," and another drawing the specious connection between Christian opposition to porn and Hitler's burning of books. *Time* magazine said the narrator's mother had helped bring in the Christian theocracy by burning porn.

At the time of the Christian revolution in the *Tale*, the "pornomarts" were shut down and "[t]here were bonfires in Times Square, crowds chanting around them, women throwing their arms up thankfully into the air when they felt the cameras on them." Atwood shows the women as only pretending to be thankful, but the young Christians as really sinister— "clean-cut stony-faced young men tossing things onto the flames" and forcing "the manufacturers and importers and salesmen" of porn to get "down on their knees" and repent in public. Thus, Atwood depicts the Christian Right as bombing lots of abortion clinics and porn shops before the revolution and then as arbitrarily and retrospectively punishing both abortionists and pornographers after the revolution. Here is an interrelated defense of abortion and pornography. Atwood warns that these two industries must stand or fall together. . . .

Covert Pornography

When we first meet Moira, she is selling porn-style lingerie at "underwhore parties" for suburban housewives trying to compete with the "Pornomarts." Atwood presents this as a clever way to earn one's way through college. Later we see Moira at the Red Center where young women are turned into handmaids—that is, made willing to serve as surrogate mothers for barren Christian women—by being shown old porn movies and told that such cruelty towards women was the result of too much "choice." Moira laughs at these movies and says the torture "wasn't real," reacting just as the narrator did, when as a child she saw the cover of the porn magazine and compared it to a Tarzan movie. Atwood wants us to believe that porn is harmless because what happens to women in porn is only entertainment. It follows from this that feminists are wrong to join the Christian Right in their anti-porn rallies. The freedom to depict perversion is intimately connected here with the freedom to have an abortion. Lose one of these freedoms and you end up, Atwood warns, in a woman-hating Christian theocracy.

In order to emphasize the harmlessness of porn and its attendant perversions, Atwood depicts her narrator as disappointed when the Commander invites her to come to his private study and she finds it is only to play Scrabble and read old magazines. At this point we are in the middle of the book, where Atwood begins to unveil her values boldly: "there had been a letdown of sorts. What had I been expecting, behind that closed door. . . . Something unspeakable, down on all fours perhaps, perversions, whips, mutilations? At the very least, some minor sexual manipulation . . . prohibited by law." Note her word *letdown*. Atwood herself once stated that her narrator in the *Tale* is "an ordinary, more-or-less cowardly woman (rather than a heroine)." Yet she would have us believe that this average, cowardly woman goes willingly and fearlessly to a place where she expects to be asked to join in sexual perversions. She would have us believe that she feels *let down* when no perversion is in sight. Surely this is why *New York Times* reviewer [Christopher] Lehmann-Haupt called the novel a cerebral sado-masochistic fantasy—not disapprovingly—and the *Socialist Review* called it a solipsistic pornographic fantasy with echoes of de Sade. For in fact, Atwood not only defends pornography in *The Handmaid's Tale*, she is covertly writing it. The link with the Marquis de Sade is worth emphasizing, for a number of feminists regard the works of de Sade in a positive light, and this pornographer may well have been the first to attack [as John Noonan wrote] "restrictions on abortion as the result of religious superstition" and exult in the "delight of destroying an embryo." . . .

A Utilitarian View of Women

Atwood wants us to believe that Christians pose a far greater threat to women than pornographers and abortionists. In her *Tale*, the Christian rulers regard women as "two-legged wombs, that's all." They see a woman beyond childbearing age or a sterile woman as having so little value that they declare her an "Unwoman" and ship her out to clean up toxic waste. And they don't provide "protective clothing" in such places because, Moira explains, these are people "they want to get rid of," especially "old women" and "Handmaids who've screwed up their three chances." The narrator's mother has been sent to sweep up toxins, and the narrator herself fears to end up there if she does not succeed in bearing a child to her third Commander. This accusation against men of the Christian Right, that they value women only for their fertility and have no other use for them, is another example of projection in this book, for who has less use for an old woman than a playboy or pornographer? But the utilitarian view of women typical of the culture of death is consistently projected here onto the culture of life. . . .

Among the perversions practiced by Christian rulers in Atwood's theocracy, the most important one is the "Ceremony." Indeed, this perversion is at the very heart of her novel, and it is described in ample and repellent detail in Chapter 16. One critic correctly calls this chapter "pornographic and voyeuristic," part of the overall "sadomasochistic fantasy." In the Ceremony, the Commander tries once a month to impregnate his handmaid as she lies in bed literally upon his wife's knees, performing his "duty" fully clothed under glaring light to avoid any hint of lust or love. This brutal Ceremony is supposedly "a literal enactment of Genesis 30:1–3," where barren Rachel gives her maid to Jacob, so that her maid may "bear upon my knees, that I may also have children by her." Indeed, the first epigraph of the *Tale* is this very passage from Genesis 30. This is strange, since no Jew or Christian in 3,000 years ever interpreted this passage as allowing three people to have intercourse at once. During the Ceremony, Atwood's narrator reflects that it is "everyone's wet dream, two women at once." Well, this is the point: the author herself tells us with a wink that the Ceremony is perversion with a biblical excuse. One critic notes shrewdly that Atwood tries to show here that sex confined to procreation is far more obscene and twisted than the perversions depicted in pornography. . . .

At the end of the novel, we learn that the Commanders have a secret brothel called Jezebel's. When the narrator discovers Moira there wearing a Playboy bunny outfit, she learns that Moira was captured and given a choice—to live the remainder of her life there or to go clean up toxic waste. The brothel is not so bad, Moira says, because it is full of women lawyers and executives who "prefer it here" to the "alternatives", so it is "Butch paradise" for her with "lots of women around." When the narrator asks if they are allowed to be lesbians, Moira emphasizes how perverted the Christian Commanders are by saying: "women on women sort of turns them on." She also declares that these Commanders enjoy bringing Handmaids to the brothel because "It's like screwing on the altar . . . your gang are supposed to be such chaste vessels." Again, Atwood is saying that Christian conservatives are the ultimate perverts.

The narrator never sees her friend again, but she hopes that Moira "blew up Jezebel's, with fifty Commanders inside it. I'd like her to end with something daring and spectacular, some outrage, something that would befit her." In these lines Atwood makes it clear that Moira is the heroine of the story—a female Samson, enslaved but indomitable, mentally unbowed, and able to bring down singlehandedly the Philistine temple of Dagon. This is her fantasy of a lesbian-feminist's revenge against the Christian Right.

A Defamation of Christian Men

Now, a tale like [George] Orwell's *1984* bears an analogy to reality. It holds the mirror up to an evil empire that once actually existed, so it works as satire. *The Handmaid's Tale* bears no such analogy to reality, not only because Christian conservatives were never on the verge of establishing a totalitarian regime in the U.S., as Atwood and her admiring reviewers have claimed, but because she gives a complete misrepresentation of the Christian Right and of the biblical view of women. For, in fact, Christian men would be the first to loathe such monsters who would exploit women for their fertility and then discard them in their old age. The projection here is very obvious. The reason why Christians oppose pornography and abortion is precisely that these industries, viewed rightly, amount to such an exploitation of women. Thus, Atwood's *Tale* does not work as satire. It is a paranoid fantasy, indeed a serious defamation of Christian men dressed up in literary style. Little wonder that *The American Atheist* gloated that Atwood had skewered American religion in this novel.

And yet, Atwood had good reason for writing this book, because the best defense is a good offense. Abortion and pornography are morally indefensible, so the best way for the supporters of these lucrative industries to claim the high moral ground is to depict their opponents as tyrannical and perverted. Such a ludicrous image of Christian conservatives, however, arises out of their own unacknowledged and unrepented guilt, which fills them with a natural fear that punishment is deserved and on the way. . . .

Contempt for Christianity and Women

In the end, *The Handmaid's Tale* is a piece of strident ideology that assaults not just the Christian Right but the Christian idea of woman. The word *handmaid* in the title alludes to the one who called herself "handmaid" when she consented to conceive and be the Mother of Christ: "I am the Handmaid of the Lord. Be it done unto me according to thy word" (Luke 1:38). For the interrelation of motherhood and chastity in the Virgin Mary and the Christian woman is at the core of the culture of life, while the interrelation of abortion and pornography has been and will continue to be at the core of the culture of death.

The Treatment of Women in *The Handmaid's Tale* Is the Historical Norm

Jill Swale

Jill Swale is the head of the Sociology Department and the coordinator of thinking and teaching strategies at Kendrick School in Reading, England. She also teaches English and sociology at Reading University and frequently contributes articles to the En-glish Review, the Sociology Review, and Teaching Thinking.

The following viewpoint offers an overview of first-wave, second-wave, and third-wave feminism, as well as postfeminism, in the Western world—specifically Canada, the United States, and Great Britain. Swale shows how these real-world political movements map to various aspects of The Handmaid's Tale. *The author points out that the subjugation of women—as illustrated in* The Handmaid's Tale—*has been common throughout history and is not strikingly different from conditions in countries such as Iran and Afghanistan.*

D espite its setting in a technologically advanced society, *The Handmaid's Tale*, according to Margaret Atwood, is not science fiction. She described its setting as 'a slight twist on the society we have now'. After discussing American right-wing Christian fundamentalism with a friend she asked her-self: 'If women's place is in the home, why aren't they in it, and how do you get them back in? And: if you were going to take over the United States, what slogans would you use?' Her ideas accumulated as she collected press cuttings about pollu-tion and the falling birth rate, and visited Afghanistan and Iran 'where women are treated in the same light as they are in Gilead's society—some ways better, some ways worse'.

Jill Swale, "Feminism and Politics in The Handmaid's Tale," *The English Review*, Sep-tember 2002, Vol. 13:1, p. 37. Copyright © 2002, Jill Swale. Reproduced by permis-sion.

She completed the novel in 1985 and set it about a decade into the future, so in a sense we might be comforted that the events described have not come to pass. Yet as time slips by and the feminist ideals of the 1970s are forgotten by new generations, there is increasing danger that a patriarchal regime similar to Gilead could arise. Since the attacks on America on 11 September 2001, and the massacre in the Indian parliament later in the year, her novel has achieved a new resonance for readers in all democratic societies: 'It was after the catastrophe, when they shot the President and machine gunned the Congress and the army declared a state of emergency. They blamed it on the Islamic fanatics at the time.' Public numbness at the scale of the tragedy and a sense of insecurity because 'there wasn't even an enemy you could put your finger on', make it easy for the new leaders of Gilead (based in Massachusetts) to introduce a totalitarian regime: 'The road blocks began to appear, and Identipasses. Everyone approved of that, since it was obvious you couldn't be too careful.'

Real-Life Gileads Around the Globe

As British readers we can identify some parallels. The introduction of identity cards, increased powers to hold suspected terrorists without trial and the censorship of inflammatory material have all been discussed by our own government since 11 September. Newspapers in Gilead are censored and closed down and people are seized by the Eyes in the street or disappear without warning, the fate of Offred's mother. In such a climate of fear and ignorance it is easy for the Gilead Commanders to introduce new laws unopposed, so that gradually most women and many men lose their human rights, supposedly as a temporary measure for the greater good. The 'Historical Notes' at the end of *The Handmaid's Tale* supply information about how the regime developed until eventually a society closer to our own re-emerged by the year 2195. It demonstrates that 'temporary' laws introduced in the early

Gilead period to alleviate the decline in the birth rate became even more stringent later. Offred is forced to become a handmaid and her child is adopted because Luke's second marriage is regarded as adulterous in the new Christian fundamentalist climate. According to Professor Pieixoto, 'In the middle period, this policy was extended to cover all marriages not contracted within the state church'.

His talk serves to add verisimilitude to the conditions in Gilead as he mentions world problems which we know to exist now, the devastation caused by AIDS and pollution of the environment. The Western birth rate really is declining, resulting in a range of measures to offset it: infertility treatments, surrogate motherhood and disastrous attempts by the former Romanian leader [Nicolae] Ceausescu to ban all birth control. Recent publicity of conditions under the Taliban in Afghanistan adds to our sense that such a society as Gilead could exist. Confinement of women to the home, the compulsory wearing of burkhas [a loose-fitting outer garment worn by women in public to keep head, face, and body covered], stringent regulations over men's lives too (such as length of beards) and the banning of secular music were all features of Afghan life bearing a strong resemblance to Gilead. Women were no longer allowed to work and female education was withdrawn, with the excuse that it was only a temporary situation. As Mullah Qallamuddin put it: 'Women must be completely segregated from men.'

Although the Taliban did not hold power in Afghanistan until after the publication of *The Handmaid's Tale*, a similar situation occurred in Iran in 1979. After the Shah was deposed and Islamic fundamentalist Ayatollah [Ruhollah] Khomeini took over, women had to don the veil, give up paid work and return to the home. Their street protests were suppressed and those who were unable to flee simply had to accept the new conditions. Members of other faiths such as Jews were persecuted and many left the country, as they were forced to do under the Gilead 'Jewish Repatriation Scheme'.

Female Subjugation Historically 'Normal'

But it was not necessary for Atwood to look to central Asia for examples of fundamentalism of an alarming kind. In North America an all-male Christian sect, the Promise Keepers [founded in 1990 in Colorado] has recently evolved which preaches that women should return to traditional roles and that strong families should be based on 'Biblical values'. There is the 'Love Can Wait' movement in which young people in mass gatherings publicly pledge themselves to chastity until marriage, and attacks on abortion clinics and the doctors who work there are fairly common. Atwood's Gilead is not as fanciful as it seems. It is an amalgam of trends which she has already observed and read about in various societies, past and present. As Pieixoto observes:

> As we know from the study of history, no new system can impose itself upon a previous one without incorporating many of the elements of the latter . . . and Gilead was no exception to this rule . . . There was little that was truly indigenous with or original to Gilead: its genius was synthesis.

Pieixoto reminds us that the freedoms experienced by women in the pre-Gilead period (the 1980s or 90s) were a mere interval between long eras of human history in which female subjugation was regarded as normal. British readers now of school age tend to take women's liberation for granted, as the teenage Offred does, but this is the very danger identified by Offred's mother and, less explicitly, by Atwood herself. It is necessary for us to examine the changing roles and status of women over a considerable period of time in order to appreciate how few rights women had in the comparatively recent past in Western societies, and how easily a backlash could remove them again. The rise of women followed a similar path in Canada, Atwood's native country, in the United States (Gilead) and in Britain. I shall focus mainly on the latter, in order to demonstrate that many of the restrictions experienced by Offred in Gilead were similar to those of ordinary British women in earlier times, and such a lifestyle is not 'science fiction'.

The Restricted Lives of Victorian Women

During the nineteenth century middle-class women were confined to the home as wives and mothers, and they were sheltered from the corrupting knowledge of the outside world. Queen Victoria said, 'Let a woman be what God intended, a helpmate for man, but with totally different duties and vocations'. Those who found this domestication tedious and protested about it were regarded as mentally disturbed 'hysterics'. Men and women were treated differently under the law. In 1857 the Matrimonial Causes Act made it far easier for men to divorce their wives than vice versa. Usually men gained all the couple's property and custody of the children after a divorce and women could be denied any access at all, especially if the wife was deemed at fault in the marriage breakdown. In Gilead, Offred's lost rights to her child are justified by a similar law, although instead of Luke it is a higher-status family which gains custody. In Britain before the Married Women's Property Act in 1870, all a woman's property became that of her husband. This happens to Offred under another Gilead law. The loss of her job also has a precedent since in Britain women had to give up many professions on marriage—this law applied to teachers until 1945.

During the Victorian period middle-class women were regarded as their husbands' possessions and were often known as the 'Angel in the House'. Their role was to be gentle, expressive homemakers. Offred alludes to this when, on losing her job, she decides to do more baking. Her radical feminist mother in contrast did not spend her time knitting or doing other feminine domestic activities, and as a child Offred rather resented this. Her mother's views were exceptional, and Offred had been socialised by a still patriarchal society to expect her mother to fulfil the traditional role which [feminist author] Betty Friedan described as 'the feminine mystique'. Though Offred is not the protagonist's original name, the reader never learns her true identity. She has become a man's possession, belonging to Fred. This method of naming is simply an extension of the Victorian tendency to refer to even eminent women, such as the writer Mrs Humphry Ward, in terms of their husbands, and for slaves to take the surnames of their owners.

In Britain women campaigned in two main historical periods, often slightly behind their North American sisters. Towards the end of the nineteenth century they campaigned for equal rights over divorce, custody of children, ownership of property, rights to university education, entry into professions such as medicine, and, most famously, for the vote. Most of the activity, known as first wave feminism, died down for a while when British women over 21 gained the vote in 1928.

Second-Wave Feminism

Women worked in greater numbers during both wars, and free nursery education was provided to enable them to do so, but withdrawn afterwards so that they would return to the home, releasing jobs for ex-servicemen. The second time this happened in 1945, women were less keen to relinquish paid work, and there were government campaigns to persuade them that it was harmful to be away from their children for long periods. [British developmental psychologist] John Bowlby was commissioned to publish a study suggesting that juvenile delinquency correlated with maternal deprivation.

However, with postwar improvements in education, many women began to resent being confined to a domestic and passive role. In 1966 the radical National Organisation for Women was formed by Betty Friedan in the United States, and in Canada the Royal Commission's Report on Women was pub-

A pamphlet from 1970 displaying leading figures of feminism's "second wave," including Ti-Grace Atkinson (upper left), Betty Friedan (lower left), and Marlene Dixon (right). © AP Photo.

lished in 1970. In Britain, consciousness-raising groups were organised to discuss women's frustrating domestic situations and their preferred roles in life. They identified gender stereotyping in literature and the media, and examined how upbringing perpetuated this situation. Some acknowledged that men, too, were forced into narrow roles. This international movement was known as second wave feminism.

Gradually these women became more politically active, campaigning for specific legal changes and opportunities. Liberal feminists sought equal pay for both sexes doing the same work, an end to discrimination in job recruitment and other spheres and good nursery provision. The first two were obtained by law in Britain in 1970 and 1975. All these recently gained rights have been lost again in Gilead.

The Exploitation of Women

Other British and American women were more militant and tended to view men as enemies. They were particularly concerned about the way female bodies were 'colonised' by men— exploited in advertising, gazed at lasciviously and harassed in the street, and, far worse, women's images comprised the major part of pornography, what is known in *The Handmaid's Tale* as 'sexploitation'. In Atwood's pre-Gilead America, this trend has become worse with the Pornomarts and Feels on Wheels. Ironically there is some truth in what the Aunts say about women being safer and less sexually exploited in hedonistic or vicious ways in Fundamentalist Gilead, except in the nightclubs which are only known to elite men. Of course the handmaids are compulsorily sexually exploited as breeding machines instead.

Other forms of exploitation of women's bodies which radical feminists in Gilead deplore are domestic violence and sexual abuse, with good reason judging from Janine's experience of gang rape. On an old film Offred's mother is seen holding a banner with the slogan 'Free the night', meaning that women should be free to walk the streets without fear of sexual attack. In pre-feminist Western societies, even within relatively happy families, men had access to women's bodies whenever they wanted, and often dictated the number of children they should have. Consultants, usually male, controlled the conditions in which women gave birth, and in Britain marital rape did not become an offence until the 1990s. Offred, even though she loves Luke, becomes aware of his power over her when she loses her job. She sees how easily this could become a threat and even holds back from lovemaking because she feels that now this has become her marital duty as his possession. She reflects on the degree to which women's lives and happiness have traditionally depended on men, and how women put huge efforts into maintaining their slim, sexually arousing appearances through fitness regimes in order to keep their man, even though it often led to exploitation. She puns, 'If you worked out enough, maybe the man would too'. Women lose out either way, either by losing men if they do not conform, or losing their independence to men if they do.

Offred's mother is one of the radical feminists who took a strong stand against the exploitation of women in the 1970s, behaving in a way which others saw as extreme in order to further the cause. She burned pornography publicly as it degraded women, wore unfeminine clothes as a form of rebellion and campaigned for women's legal right to abortion, obtained in Britain in 1967. Although she had a child she did not wish to be legally tied to the father, preferring the company of women whom she could trust more. In the 1970s sisterhood was important to campaigners, some of whom moved to feminist communes where they lived either as lesbians, as Moira did, or led celibate lives. Feminist writers even recommended artificial insemination by sperm bank so that babies could be born without the father trying to exert ownership over the mother and child. This meant that women's bodies were under their own control, in contrast to the fate of Offred in Gilead for whom biology is destiny. In the bath to prepare her for 'the Ceremony' with the Commander she laments, "I don't want to look at something which determines me so completely." Offred's body is linked with a prize pig's, a chicken waiting to be tenderised and an open tulip. These are reminders of the way patriarchal societies have equated women with nature, whereas many of them wish to connect with culture and intellectual life, represented by the forbidden Scrabble and books in the Commander's study.

Third-Wave Feminism and Postfeminism

In the West the second feminist movement is now regarded as over by most sociologists. Middle-class women have become complacent as they have gained most of the legal changes they sought in the 1960s and 70s. Women in other parts of the world are still grossly exploited through forced marriages, genital mutilation, sexual slavery and educational discrimination—movements addressing these issues are known as third wave feminism. Here, and in America, there has been a reaction against feminism, documented in Susan Faludi's [1991 book] *Backlash*. Books by male writers such as Neil Lyndon have argued that women's rights now exceed men's, and organisations like 'Families Need Fathers' have sprung up in male defence. Some argue that women's desire to 'have it all', both career and family life, has led to stress, child neglect and family breakdown. The media have been keen to focus on mothers who have given up high-powered careers to return to the home. Younger women seem to have little interest in feminism, taking their opportunities for granted and not realising that they could easily be lost again. This state of affairs is referred to as post-feminism.

Offred's mother warns of the dangers of complacency and prophetically tells her daughter, 'History will absolve me'. Moira, another radical feminist, realises that women's rights are precarious and is unsurprised when they are tricked out of their money and jobs. Offred herself represents the present generation of young American women, well-educated, wanting a career, but rather scathing of feminism, valuing romantic love and somewhat traditional in some of her thinking. At-wood deliberately chose such a person as an Everywoman with whom the reader can identify. She said, 'The voice is that of an ordinary, more-or-less cowardly woman (rather than a heroine), because I am more interested in social history than in the biographies of the outstanding'.

The novel is undoubtedly a warning to women, but its message extends beyond that to all people to avoid the dangers of the political apathy in which totalitarian regimes flourish.

The Handmaid's Tale Dramatizes the 1980s Antifeminist Backlash

Shirley Neuman

Shirley Neuman is a Canadian academic and professor. She was the founding chair of the University of Alberta's Women's Studies Program and is also a former dean of the University of Michigan's College of Literature, Science, and the Arts.

From the early twentieth century through the 1970s, various feminist movements made great gains in securing equal rights and social standing for American women. Subsequently, in the 1980s there was a simultaneous backlash against feminism—which political and cultural conservatives claimed had gone too far and thus disrupted the "natural" balance between the genders—and a surge in postfeminist sentiment, the notion that feminism had succeeded in leveling the playing field and thus was no longer necessary. In this viewpoint, the author argues that the Gilead of The Handmaid's Tale *is both a product of the backlash—in that it is founded by those who so strenuously argued against feminist gains in the 1980s—and a solution to the social dangers (kidnapping, murder, rape, loneliness, divorce, despair) that filled the vacuum left when the movement to secure universal equality was abandoned.*

Margaret Atwood conceived the Republic of Gilead in *The Handmaid's Tale* as one logical outcome of what she termed the 'strict theocracy' of the 'fundamentalist government' of the United States' Puritan founding fathers. Her Gileadean government maintains its power by means of

Shirley Neuman, "'Just a Backlash': Margaret Atwood, Feminism, and *The Handmaid's Tale*," *University of Toronto Quarterly*, Summer 2006, Vol. 75:3, pp. 857–868. Copyright © 2006, University of Toronto Quarterly. Reproduced by permission.

surveillance, suppression of information, 're-education' centres, and totalitarian violence. Its major national issue, sterility consequent on nuclear and chemical pollution, it addresses through sexual surrogacy, turning its few fertile women into 'Handmaids' to its highest-level Commanders and their wives, using as justification the biblical story in which the barren Rachel directs her husband Jacob to 'go in unto' her servant Billah: 'and she shall bear upon my knees, that I also may have children by her' (epigraph).

We learn about Gilead through one of its (self-described) 'two-legged wombs' or 'ambulatory chalices,' the Handmaid Offred, who records her story after she has escaped the regime. Caught up in a dystopian state that the novel hypothesizes as the logical extension not only of Puritan government but also of the agenda articulated during the 1980s by America's fundamentalist Christian Right, what Offred knows is that power pervades every aspect of Gileadean life. Power: 'who can do what to whom and get away with it, even as far as death,' 'who can do what to whom and be forgiven for it.' What Offred also knows is that the temptations of power offer a feminine inflection: 'if you happen to be a man,' she addresses her future reader, 'and you've made it this far, please remember: you will never be subjected to the temptation of feeling you must forgive, a man, as a woman.' The novel's outwardly conformist and once independent Offred has seen her social value reduced to reproduction, and her personal freedom completely curtailed. But the retrospective monologue in which she tells her story reveals her as observant of the gendered configurations of power in both the personal and the political realms, in both 'the time before' and the present of the novel. It also shows her as analytic and ironic about those relations and as capable of using them to her own advantage. Offred, in short, is a fictional product of 1970s feminism, and she finds herself in a situation that is a fictional realization of the backlash against women's rights that gathered force during the early 1980s.

Roots of the Antifeminist Backlash

Between 1965, when Atwood wrote her first published novel, *The Edible Woman*, and 1985 when she published *The Handmaid's Tale*, women—especially middle-class women like Atwood's heroines—had seen major improvements in their access to higher education and the professions, in employment equity, in access to legal abortion, and in divorce law. Atwood herself had been embraced as a feminist novelist by a panoply of writers and critics representing a wide variety of feminist positions. She had responded initially by resisting the label *feminist* (a label that she noted was sometimes used by reviewers to dismiss her early work), then by carefully defining the kind of feminist she was. By 1976, she described herself as 'probably . . . a feminist, in the broad sense of the term', but in a 1979 interview she also found the term insufficiently 'inclusive' of her interests. When *The Handmaid's Tale* was about to appear, Atwood gave an interview to feminist theorist Elizabeth Meese, in which she iterated her definition of feminism as a 'belief in the rights of women . . . [as] equal human beings' but in which she also firmly distanced herself from feminist or doctrinaire separatism: she would have no truck with attempts—feminist or otherwise—to control what people write or say, and 'if practical, hardline, anti-male feminists took over and became the government, I would resist them'. She had put the matter more positively two years earlier, just before she turned to the writing of *The Handmaid's Tale*: 'Am I a propagandist? No! Am I an observer of society? Yes! And no one who observes society can fail to make observations that are feminist. That is just . . . commonsense.'

Such a commonsense observer, alert in the years between 1965 and 1985, could not have helped but see a world that, if still far from perfect, looked to be getting better and better for women. Nor could an alert observer have helped but notice that, for some, the world seemed to be getting a little too free for women. Atwood, like many feminists of the period, was keenly aware of the fragility of the newly acquired rights and equalities of women: of the opposition to these rights and equalities in many quarters, of the many places and ways in which these gains were threatened or actively eroded, and of the intersection of women's issues, feminist issues, and broader human rights issues.

By 1984, the year in which pundits looked back on George Orwell's dystopia [titled *Nineteen Eighty-Four*] to assess how much of his vision we had escaped and also the year in which Margaret Atwood sat down to write *The Handmaid's Tale*, both totalitarianism and those who hoped to retrench some of the gains of feminism had made significant inroads on the successes of the 1970s. Atwood kept a file of these inroads on human rights and women's freedom, which she took with her on book tours as evidence for her insistence that she had 'invented nothing' in Gilead. If Gilead is, in the logic of the novel, one possible extension of the real world of 1984, we can understand something of the impulse to its creation and of the character of Offred by briefly recollecting early 1980s reactions to the successes of the women's movement as well as the intersections of these reactions with some of the totalitarian excesses of the period.

Women Lose Rights in the 1980s

By 1984, Ayatollah Khomeini had forced women out of Iranian universities, out of their jobs, and back into their *burqas* [a loose-fitting outer garment worn by women in public to keep head, face, and body covered] and their homes. Iranian prison refugees reported torture including the use of electric prods and frayed steel cables in beatings, and such a report by one woman found its way into Atwood's file. In Afghanistan, as Atwood herself observed, 'Thinking that it's O.K. for women to read and write would be a radically feminist position.' And, as Professor Pieixoto reminds us in the novel's epilogue, the

Philippines, under the rubric of 'salvaging,' engaged in state-sanctioned murder of dissidents, while [Nicolae] Ceausescu's government in Romania monitored women monthly for pregnancy, outlawed birth control and abortion, and linked women's wages to childbearing. The professor appears to have read Atwood's file: both these precedents for the actions of Gilead had found their way into her clippings documenting her assertion that she had invented nothing in Gilead.

By 1984, in the United States, the gains women had achieved during the previous decade had come under attack from several directions. During Ronald Reagan's presidency [1981–1989], women made up an increasing percentage of those in the lowest-paid occupations, and they made no gains or lost ground in the better-paid trades and professions. The number of elected and politically appointed women declined. One-third of all federal budget cuts under Reagan's presidency came from programs that served mainly women, even though these programs represented only 10 per cent of the federal budget. The average amount a divorced man paid in child support fell 25 per cent. Murders related to sexual assault and domestic violence increased by 160 per cent while the overall murder rate declined; meanwhile the federal government defeated bills to fund shelters for battered women, stalled already approved funding, and in 1981 closed down the Office of Domestic Violence it had opened only two years earlier. Pro-natalists [antiabortion activists] bombed and set fire to abortion clinics and harassed their staff and patients; Medicaid ceased to fund legal abortions, effectively eliminating freedom of choice for most teenage girls and poor women; several states passed laws restricting not only legal abortion but even the provision of information about abortion. The debate about freedom of choice for women flipped over into court rulings about the rights and freedom of the fetus. The Equal Rights Amendment died.

The Fall of Feminism

By 1984, the American New Right had metamorphosed into Jerry Falwell's Moral Majority. Televangelists, some of them at home in the White House, told their congregations that 'feminists encourage women to leave their husbands, kill their children, practice witchcraft, destroy capitalism and become lesbians' (letter of Pat Robertson to his congregation) and that AIDS was divine retribution for the 'sin' of homosexuality. Right-wing wives such as best-selling Phyllis Schlafly made a handsome income telling other women to return home, to let their husbands provide, and to use their femininity and feminine wiles as the core of their success and fulfilment as women. Schlafly put forward Katharine Hepburn as a role model—not Hepburn the successful actress to be sure, but Hepburn at the feet of Spencer Tracy, 'submissive and more abnegating than any wife this side of the Orient.' Several readers identify Schlafly as the prototype of Aunt Lydia at the 'Red,' or reeducation, Centre of *The Handmaid's Tale* and of her 'implicit' advice to the Handmaids: 'Men are sex machines . . . and not much more. . . . You must learn to manipulate them, for your own good. . . . It's nature's way. It's God's device. It's the way things are.' Others find in her the prototype for the Commander's wife, Serena Joy, of whom Offred ironically observes, 'She stays in her home, but it doesn't seem to agree with her. How furious she must be, now that she's been taken at her word.'

In 1984, the 'most popular talk show' in the United States was hosted by Rush Limbaugh, who used it as a platform from which to attack what he called 'femi-Nazi[s].' The media began to announce that the world had moved into a 'post-feminist' era, while at the same time it gave wide circulation to a number of badly designed, badly analysed, badly misrepresented, or dishonestly co-opted studies claiming to prove that single career women had high rates of neuroses and unhappiness, that women's incomes declined an average of 70 per cent post-divorce, that the United States was in the grip of an 'infertility epidemic,' that a professional woman over thirty was about as likely to win a lottery jackpot as to find a man. Across North America, young women in universities, in the confidence born of their mothers' success, in the desire for self-differentiation that ever characterizes the young, overly credulous of the media and perhaps anxious to find a man, asserted that they didn't need feminism.

Offred, in 'the time before' of *The Handmaid's Tale*, is one such young woman, sceptical of and embarrassed by her mother's feminist activism, which includes 'Take Back the Night' marches, bonfires of pornography, and planned single motherhood. 'As for you,' her mother tells her, 'you're just a backlash. . . . You young people don't appreciate things. . . . You don't know what we had to go through, just to get you where you are. Look at him,' pointing to her son-in-law, 'slicing up the carrots. Don't you know how many women's lives, how many women's *bodies*, the tanks had to roll over just to get that far?' . . .

Offred's Transformation

Reading the novel, we spend a great deal of time inside Offred's head. And Offred spends a great deal of time not only remembering 'the time before' and observing the circumstances of her present, but also commenting on both. Her commentary is often ironic, often analytic, often critical of herself and of her peers in 'the time before.' It also shows her as having gained political awareness and as reassessing her earlier more individualist positions. In her thoughts, for example, she engages in a rich dialogue with her mother, recollecting her earlier negative reactions to her mother's feminist activism but also learning to acknowledge some of the ways in which her mother was right. . . .

Remembering this past, . . . Offred concludes that 'I took too much for granted; I trusted fate, back then.' As her story

President Ronald Reagan (left) shakes hands with Jerry Falwell, cofounder of the conservative Christian political group the Moral Majority, on January 30, 1984. © AP Photo/Ira Schwarz.

unfolds she becomes tougher on her earlier life: 'We lived,' she says, 'by ignoring. Ignoring isn't the same as ignorance, you have to work at it. . . . There were stories in the newspapers, of course, corpses in ditches or the woods, bludgeoned to death or mutilated, interfered with as they used to say, but they were about other women, and the men who did such things were other men. . . . We lived in the gaps between the stories.' Her willed ignorance anaesthetizes any impulse to resist the increasingly repressive actions leading to the coup that establishes Gilead. When a strange woman attempts to abduct her child, Offred works at ignoring: 'I thought it was an isolated incident, at the time.' When the Pornomarts and the mobile brothels on Harvard Square suddenly disappear, she fails to challenge a sales clerk's apathetic comment: 'Who knows, who cares' what happened to them. And when all women are told they no longer have a job, she asks, 'What was it about this that made us feel we deserved it?' Willed ignorance, Offred learns, is sister to victimization and to passive acceptance of blame for what is done to one.

In Gilead, Offred decides against being a victim: 'I intend to last,' she declares. To last, she must pay attention. Especially early on in the novel, she is alert to every detail around her. Some of her observation is undertaken to fill the time, as when she minutely inspects every corner of her room. Some of it is a device to distance herself from the horror of her situation: 'One detaches oneself. One describes,' she remarks as the Commander does his 'duty' on the lower half of her body in the 'Rachel' ceremony, or as she lays her hand on the rope about to hang two women. Most of her attention is in aid of survival. Entering the Commander's household, meeting her shopping companion Ofglen for the first time, she pays the closest heed to the smallest gestures of everyone around her, 'reading' them constantly. 'Watch out, Commander, I tell him in my head. I've got my eye on you. One false move and I'm dead.'

The measure of the distance Offred has travelled, by means of attentiveness, from her willed ignorance in 'the time before' comes when she gains some small power over the Commander as a consequence of having read the signs of what happened to the Handmaid before her. When she once would have worked to ignore those signs, she now seeks knowledge. Asked what she would like, she responds, 'I would like to know. . . . Whatever there is to know. What's going on.'

Survival Is Complicity with Oppression

We must be wary, however, of the impulse to make an unmitigated heroine of the novel's Offred. Her desire to survive and to know comes with a necessary degree of complicity and a tendency to relapse. In her new self-awareness, Offred specifically accepts the element of complicitous choice in her situation. Lying on her back, she reasons: 'Nor does rape cover it: nothing is going on here that I haven't signed up for. There wasn't a lot of choice but there was some, and this is what I chose.' She also recognizes and acknowledges her enjoyment of her own small exercises of power, however ignoble: her sexual teasing of the Guardians at the checkpoint, her slight power not only over the Commander, because he wants something from her, but over his wife, whom they are deceiving. She comes to understand that the Commander craves some unspoken forgiveness for the conditions of her life and that to bestow or to withhold forgiveness is 'a power, perhaps the greatest,' as well as a temptation. 'How easy it is to invent a humanity, for anyone at all,' she reflects, thinking of the Commander's request that she play Scrabble in the same breath as she recollects an interview with the mistress of one of the supervisors of a concentration camp. . . .

The personal is political . . . , just as feminism had already told us. . . . Nowhere is the personal more political than in Gilead, where the very choice of becoming a Handmaid or a Jezebel over going to the Colonies to sweep up radioactive waste signals a degree of complicity with the regime and where playing a game of Scrabble with the Commander renders him both human and comic. Nowhere more so than in Gilead, where each Handmaid must pull the rope to tighten its noose around the necks of state-murdered women. Nowhere more so than in Gilead, where the Handmaids accept the party line that the men given them to kill in 'particicutions' are rapists and where Offred acknowledges her own 'bloodlust; I want to tear, gouge, rend.'

If Offred's survival depends on attention and on astute choices about complicity, her affair with Nick marks a relapse into willed ignorance. Readers have tended to identify strongly with the sense of connection and renewed sexuality Offred discovers in her relationship with Nick and to understand this couple in light of the conventions of the romance plot, in which the male lover rescues the hapless heroine. Atwood is, I would argue, telling us something else. There is no evidence in the novel that Nick's 'rescue' of Offred is motivated by anything other than self-preservation. In the world of sexual relationships, after all, his final words, 'Trust me,' are as clichéd and unreliable as the Commander's explanation that his wife doesn't understand him or as Serena Joy's final reproach as Offred is hustled out the door: 'After all he did for you.' Most importantly, when Offred falls under the spell of her rendezvous with Nick, she no longer wishes to escape and she no longer wants to know from Ofglen what is going on. Her relapse into willed ignorance partly motivates the shame that so strongly marks her narrative at this point. She has ceased, she realizes as she sees the dreaded black van arrive for her at the end of the novel, 'to pay attention.'

Utopia Implicit in Every Dystopia

In dystopias, the present is co-opted to evil ends, driven to one logical (though not inevitable) conclusion, its understandings and language perverted. In dystopias, Handmaids greet each other with words from the Catholic litany to the Virgin, 'Blessed be the fruit,' while the state hangs priests. In dystopias clichés from 'the time before' signal both normalcy and extreme differences of power. In dystopias, the call of some radical feminists for a 'woman's culture' becomes the birthing scene of *The Handmaid's Tale* or the brothel called Jezebel's. In dystopias, the doxology of the Christian fundamentalist Right that would return women to their homes to fulfil their putative biological destiny is realized by a Handmaid lying between a wife's legs in a parody of the biblical story of Rachel and her servant Billah.

But also implicit in every dystopia is a utopia. As Atwood herself observed, 'we the readers are to deduce what a good society is by seeing what it isn't.' And here some readers of *The Handmaid's Tale* . . . have misread the novel by conflating Offred's desire to have 'everything back, the way it was' with Atwood's implicit utopia. I quote John Updike in his egregiously nostalgic *New Yorker* review: 'among [the novel's] cautionary and indignant messages, Miss Atwood has threaded a curious poem to the female condition. Offred's life of daily waiting and shopping, of timorous strategizing and sudden bursts of daring, forms an intensified and darkened version of a woman's customary existence, a kind of begrimed window through which glimpses of Offred's old, pre-Gilead life—its work and laughter and minor dissipations, its female friends and husband and child, its costumes and options—flicker with the light of paradise.' The novel, he concludes, 'is suffused . . . by the author's lovely subversive hymn to our ordinary life, as lived, amid perils and pollution, now.' Updike is working hard at willed ignorance.

Bearing Witness to the Backlash

For what does *The Handmaid's Tale* . . . tell us about 'the time before' by means of Offred's memories, Aunt Lydia's lectures, and the Commander's rationalizations? It tells us that one's husband could slice the carrots for dinner, that one could live with him and one's daughter and cat and argue and banter with one's mother and friends in an easy, loving intimacy, yes.

But it also tells us that it was not safe for a woman to go for a run or into a laundromat at night, to open the door to a stranger, to help a stranded motorist; that women didn't walk in certain places, locked doors and windows, drew curtains, left lights on as precautions or perhaps 'prayers'; that women needed to 'take back the night' and to replace kitchen-table abortions with legal freedom of choice; that date rape was common enough to be an accepted subject for a term paper; that pornography, including snuff movies, was a fact of life that women were 'found—often women but sometimes they would be men, or children, that was the worst—in ditches or forests or refrigerators in abandoned rented rooms, with their clothes on or off, sexually abused or not; at any rate killed'; that one did not allow one's children to walk alone to school because too many disappeared; that less terminally lethal circumstances included singles bars, blind dates, 'the terrible gap between the ones who could get a man easily and the ones who couldn't' as well as a dedication to anorexia, silicone implants, and cosmetic surgery as means to realize the 'possibilities' proffered by fashion magazines; that fathers left without paying child support, mothers wound up on welfare, and the 'wretched little paycheques' of women would have to stretch to unsubsidized daycare.

The implicit women's utopia of *The Handmaid's Tale* is not in 'the time before.' It exists outside the 'either/or' thinking so beloved of Aunt Lydia, and outside the novel: outside of the dangers, humiliations, inequities, and backlash that women experience in its 'time before,' but also outside totalitarian Gilead's claims to have improved their lot. A first step to utopia, Atwood's novel tells us, requires that we 'pay attention' and bear witness, as does Offred when she uses her uncertain freedom to tell her story.

Feminism and Religious Fundamentalism Merge in *The Handmaid's Tale*

Barbara Ehrenreich

Barbara Ehrenreich is an author, feminist, and liberal political activist. She is best known for her reporting on social and economic inequality in the United States and worldwide, especially for her detailed explorations of how these affect the lives of women.

Written in 1986, this viewpoint is anchored in both the culture that The Handmaid's Tale *satirizes (the increasingly culturally conservative America of the 1980s postfeminist backlash) and the culture that Atwood has most clearly spoken to (the educated liberal democrats). Ehrenreich argues that Atwood's horror tale of a conservative future highlights the identical totalitarian leanings at the heart of both the extreme conservative right, represented by the government of Gilead, and the extreme liberal feminist left, embodied by Offred's pornography-burning mother and radical friend Moira.*

The feminist imagination has been far more productive of utopias (from Charlotte Perkins Gilman's *Herland* to Marge Piercy's *Woman on the Edge of Time*) than of dystopias, and for good reason. Almost every thinkable insult to women has been tested and institutionalized at one time or another: foot-binding, witch-burning, slavery, organized rape, ritual mutilation, enforced childbearing, enforced chastity, and the mere denial of ordinary rights to own property, speak out in public, or walk down a street without fear. For misogynist nastiness, it is hard to improve on history.

Yet there has been no shortage of paranoid folklore about what the future may hold for women. Since the early 1970s, one important strand of feminist thought (usually called "cultural" or "radical" feminist) has tended to see all of history as a male assault on women and, by proxy, on nature itself. Hence rape, hence acid rain, hence six-inch high heels, hence the arms race, hence (obviously) the scourge of pornography. Extrapolating from this miserable record, cultural feminists have foreseen women being driven back to servitude as breeders and scullery maids, or else, when reproductive technology is refined enough to make wombs unnecessary, being eliminated altogether. The alternative, they believe, is to create a "women's culture," envisioned as intrinsically loving, nurturing, and in harmony with nature—before we are all destroyed by the toxic effects of testosterone.

A Mundane and Horrifying Future

Margaret Atwood's new novel is being greeted as the long-awaited feminist dystopia, and I am afraid that for some time it will be viewed as a test of the imaginative power of feminist paranoia. Is Atwood's brave new world really so bad? Is it as ingeniously awful as [George Orwell's dystopia] *1984*? And, by implication, are the fears—or for that matter, the concerns—of feminism worth taking all that seriously? Atwood's book has, for better or worse, taken the most obvious route from here to hell: the Moral Majority, or some group of similar persuasion, has taken over the United States, extirpated the printed word, hunted down the heretics, and established a medieval-style theocracy that is almost as boring, in a day-to-day sense, as it is grisly.

It is not only women who are in trouble in the new Christian nation. The "Children of Ham" are being relocated from the cities to their new "homeland" in North Dakota. Jews have been packed aboard ships supposedly headed for Israel. It's open season on Catholics, Quakers, former abortionists, and "gender traitors" (male homosexuals), all of whom are likely to end up hung from hooks on the wall that runs along the city of Gilead. But women are in a particularly tight spot. Some combination of plagues and toxic waste has decimated the human gene pool, so that women who may still have the potential to bear children have been pressed into service as full-time breeders, or "handmaids." A handmaid's job is to service a "Commander" and, indirectly, his usually sterile, aging wife, in a lewd little ménage à trois justified by the scriptural arrangement between the childless Rachel and her maid Bilhah.

What we see through the eyes of the handmaid narrator, Offred (of-Fred, her current Commander), is mostly the narrow household in which she must mate once a month, and wait passively for signs of pregnancy. The real power in the household lies with the regally blue-robed Wife, who was in the old days, we are pleased to learn, a celebrated right-wing evangelical TV personality, and is now festering with resentment at a world in which women are barred from any visible public role. There are also two servants, genetically called "Marthas" and consigned to dull green outfits, and a cocky chauffeur called Nick, who may or may not be an "Eye," a spy for the central authorities, whoever they are. And, as in *1984*, there is a resistance movement, which Offred learns of through a handmaid in a neighboring household; but, also as in *1984*, the only truly subversive force appears to be love. Fred, the bumbling, wistful Commander, falls in love with Offred, who in turn falls for the inscrutable Nick.

A Dimly Drawn Future

It is not the plot, however, or even the novel social setting, which accounts for the peculiar grip of *The Handmaid's Tale*. Atwood has woven a fantasy of regression that is almost as seductive, in a perverse way, as it is repellent. Offred had been a happy yuppie in "the time before," with a husband, a daughter, a job, money to spend, decisions to make, and of course, a name of her own. Now her only responsibility is to conceive; otherwise it is to sit quietly and stare out through a window of shatter-proof glass. There is not much to think about except the time of the month and the next meal, which will invariably feature soft bland offerings like canned pears and milk. Offred cries a lot and lives in fear of finding her erstwhile husband hanging from a hook on the wall, but when she is finally contacted by the resistance, she is curiously uninterested. She has sunk too far into the incestuous little household she serves—just as the reader, not without intermittent spasms of resistance, sinks into the deepening masochism of her tale.

My own resistance came from wanting to know more about this nightmare world, much more than Offred cares to find out. As a dystopia, this is a thinly textured one; and it is hard to know whether to blame the author or the narrator, who is forced, after all, into a kind of tunnel vision by the wimple she must wear along with her red handmaid's uniform. Offred spends a lot of time on aimless mental word games: "I sit in the chair and think about the word *chair*. It can also mean the leader of a meeting. It can also mean a mode of execution. It is the first syllable in *charity*," and so forth.

Maybe this is how people think when they are depressed and have nothing to read. Still, one yearns for a narrator with a little anthropological imagination. Who is in charge here? Is there still a central government? The consumer culture has been almost obliterated, but has capitalism itself been routed by the fundamentalists? And if printed matter is illegal, what do they do without operating manuals for the cars and computers that are still very much in use? Yet when Offred finally rouses herself to put a question to the Commander, all she can come up with is a weak request to know "whatever there is to know. . . . What's going on."

Still from a 1990 film adaptation of The Handmaid's Tale, *directed by Volker Schlöndorff.*
© Photos 12/Alamy.

The Merging of Liberals and Conservatives

But if Offred is a sappy stand-in for [Orwell's protagonist] Winston Smith, and Gilead seems at times to be only a coloring book version of [*Nineteen Eighty-Four's*] Oceania, it may be because Atwood means to do more than scare us about the obvious consequences of a Falwellian coup d'état [i.e., a government takeover by the likes of 1980s Christian Right leader the Reverend Jerry Falwell]. There is a subtler argument at work in *The Handmaid's Tale* and it is as intellectually interesting as the fictional world she has housed it in. We are being warned, in this tale, not only about the theocratic ambitions of the religious right, but about a repressive tendency in feminism itself. Only on the surface is Gilead a fortress of patriarchic Old Testament style. It is also, in a thoroughly sinister and distorted way, the utopia of cultural feminism.

There is, for example, no pornography in the new world (even the Bible is kept under lock and key); there are no cosmetics or other artifices to insult the natural female form, and the punishment for rape is to be torn to bits by a mob of women. Men, including physicians, have been barred from the scene of childbirth which is now assisted by a ritual circle of chanting handmaids. In the Red Center where handmaids are trained for service the presiding "Aunts" indoctrinate their charges in a twisted proto-feminist ideology: women were once subject to hideous abuse by men, but now they are "free" from all that, while men have been reduced, for all practical purposes to stud service. Aunt Lydia even offers oblique praise for the more separatist feminists of our own time, and dreams of a future in which "Women will live in harmony with each other . . . Women united for a common end!" The irony is not lost on Offred, whose own mother had been something of a feminist termagant, fond of pornographic book burnings. "You wanted a women's culture" Offred thinks, addressing her mother. "Well, now there is one. It isn't what you meant, but it exists."

Revolutionaries seldom do get exactly what they want, but at least with *The Handmaid's Tale* we stand warned. There has been an ominous convergence between some of the ideas of the antifeminist right and those of the cultural feminist militants. The antifeminists would like to get us all back to the kitchen, but they are also responsible for some of the most strident female supremacist literature to come out of the last two decades' gender wars. (See, for example, Phyllis Schlafly's *The Power of The Positive Woman*.) The cultural feminists, for their part, would like women to be free agents in the public sphere, but other feminists argue that their views on sex may be ultimately repressive to women. On the issue of pornography, the two sides appear to agree wholeheartedly, although just what it is, and whether it might even be defined to include a thoroughly feminist nightmare like *The Handmaid's Tale*, no one can say.

This tale is an absorbing novel, as well as an intra feminist polemic. Still, it does remind us that, century after century, women have been complicit in their own undoing. Like the sadistic Aunts in *The Handmaid's Tale*, it was women who bound their granddaughters' feet, women who turned over their little girls for clitoridectomies [female genital mutilation], and often even women who denounced their neighbors as witches. In the long sorry story of human cruelty and pillage, women are actors as well as victims, even when, like Offred, we choose to turn our backs and burrow into the narrow world of daily life. We can do better—we *have* to do better, because that hard rain or toxic waste will fall not only on those who conspired to torture nature, but on those who merely swooned and simpered.

The Special Impact
of *The Handmaid's Tale*
on Female Readers

J. Brooks Bouson

J. Brooks Bouson is a professor of English at Loyola University of Chicago. Bouson's teaching and research interests include twentieth-century women's literature, psychoanalysis and litera- ture, feminist theory, and the history of feminist criticism.

Drawn from the collection Approaches to Teaching Atwood's "The Handmaid's Tale" and Other Works, *this viewpoint spe- cifically addresses the use of Atwood's novel in the classroom and the profound emotional impact the book has on many female readers. The author points out that this is magnified by Offred's metaphorical role as the Commander's daughter, struggling with the jealousy of his Wife, as well as by Atwood's detailed explora- tion of how compromised the Handmaids are in their capacity to consent to, or rail against, their confinement. The novel's con- clusion, which at once mimics the common tropes of the ro- mance novel yet refuses to conclusively reveal whether or not Of- fred "gets saved"—by a heroic man, or otherwise—creates further uncomfortable tension for female readers.*

Commenting that when she reads a woman writer, she feels she is "reading something closer to home," Margaret Atwood admits that "things that are closer to home have the power to make you a lot more nervous and anxious than things that are more remote." As I have discovered in teaching *The Handmaid's Tale* at a women's college to both traditional-age and returning adult students, Atwood's novel has the power to make women readers anxious. And it also brings home the truth of the dictum that for women "the personal is political."

An Agonizing Read for Women

Despite *The Handmaid's Tale*'s painful subject matter, many of my women students report in their response statements that they feel compelled to read the novel. "I could barely put the book down," one student comments. "I was riveted to it with terror and pain. When I would put the book down, I'd have to force myself to get back to reality." Another student, who describes *The Handmaid's Tale* as "one of the most fascinating and compelling novels" she had ever read, remarks that she became "so wrapped up in" the novel that she found it difficult to "put the novel down," and she felt she was "alongside" Offred, "experiencing everything" that Atwood's character was "going through." Since women readers can readily identify with Offred, and since their own, often unacknowledged, anxieties about sexual exploitation may be stirred by Atwood's novel, reading *The Handmaid's Tale* can be an emotionally wrenching experience for many student-readers. "I felt disgust, anger, fear, and sadness while reading this novel," remarks one student. "I became outraged for Offred but at the same time defeated with her," writes another student.

Responding with great passion to the plight of Atwood's character, students also pay heed to the political implications of *The Handmaid's Tale*. "It literally gave me chills not only to read this story but to really believe that something like this can happen [in the United States]," comments a student who "did not believe for a minute" that Atwood's novel was "pure fantasy." Aware of the conservative backlash against feminism and the political agenda of the New Right fundamentalists, she found it difficult to dismiss the book. "I'm fearful that in many subtle ways some similar things are already happening; I'm frustrated and angry, and I don't know what to do with these overwhelming feelings." "Once the remote possibility of Offred's fate is internalized by the reader, it becomes necessary to take time out to consider the magnitude of it," writes another student. "This incredibly sterile, oppressed society is not beyond rational comprehension given the realities of Nazi Germany, for example. It is an extremely unsettling realization that such a fate could actually befall contemporary women."

The Female Oedipal Psychological Drama

Because *The Handmaid's Tale* provokes such a passionate response from women students, who are anxious to talk about and make sense of what they have experienced, I find it easy to lead them into a more formal discussion of the feminist and psychoanalytic concerns at the thematic center of the novel. To help situate students, I provide an overview of [Sigmund] Freud's theory of female development, focusing particular attention on the oedipal drama, in which the girl becomes attached to her father and views her mother as a rival for the father's affection. I begin my analysis of *The Handmaid's Tale* by concentrating on the novel's family—and female oedipal—drama, showing how the novel makes visible the pattern of desire laid down during female oedipal development and how it stages the female oedipal fantasy, in which the girl wishes to take the place of the mother and marry the father. "If female readers of a particular culture share certain fantasies, it is because particular child-raising patterns, shared across a culture, embed common fantasy structures in their daughters," remarks Jean Wyatt. Not only are family relations "the principal conduits between cultural ideology and the individual unconscious," but cultural ideology "is most subtle and insidious when it comes in the form of interpersonal relations in the family." In female oedipal development, the daughter's relationship to her father "trains her to idealize a distant and mysterious figure whose absences she can fill with glamorous projections." Some of the behaviors that "speak directly to the quirks of a female unconscious patterned by life in a patriarchal family are waiting, flirting, and the oedipal triangle," writes Wyatt. Because the "father's homecoming" is the "exciting event of a child's day," the waiting daughter comes to associate novelty and stimulation with the arrival of the father—a behavior that is repeated later in the romance scenario in which "lover and waiting woman assume the active and passive roles first played out by father and daughter." Enacting an important developmental role by "diverting his daughter's erotic impulses, first oriented toward her mother, into heterosexual channels," the father also engages in "sexual flirtation" with the daughter but does not follow through because of the incest taboo.

Providing a thinly disguised dramatization of the female oedipal situation, in which the daughter views the mother as a rival and is drawn to the father, *The Handmaid's Tale*, as I point out to my students, presents Serena Joy as a "malicious and vengeful woman" and the Commander as "not an unkind man." And the narrative also enacts the "waiting" and "flirting" behavior typical of the father-daughter relationship. When asked to meet secretly with the Commander in his study, Offred finds that these visits give her "something to do" and "to think about" and thus relieve the tedium of her life of passive waiting. But she also realizes that she is "only a whim" for the Commander, who likes it when she distinguishes herself, showing "precocity, like an attentive pet, prick-eared and eager to perform.... [H]e is positively daddyish. He likes to think I am being entertained; and I am, I am." But what is culturally repressed in this developmental scenario—because of the taboo against incest—is acted out in the novel's staging of the monthly insemination ceremony.

The Text Victimizes Female Readers

In essence victimizing readers by positioning them as voyeurs and subjecting them to the obscene spectacle of the Ceremony, the narrative partially conceals what it reveals as it minimizes the horror of what is being described. For Offred protectively distances herself from what she is experiencing: she "detaches" herself, she "describes," she finds "something hilarious" about the impregnation ritual. Similarly, at least one critic claims to find a "humorous correspondence" between Atwood's description of the Ceremony and its biblical source in the Rachel and Bilhah story alluded to in one of the epigraphs to the novel. If readers, in being encouraged to locate the connections between the Gileadean Ceremony and its biblical counterpart, participate in the narrative's defenses, this pornographic—and voyeuristic—scene is, nevertheless, profoundly disturbing. The fact that students typically omit direct references to the Ceremony in their response statements and are uncomfortable discussing it in class reveals just how disturbing this central scene is.

As Offred lies between the legs of the Commander's Wife, "my head on her stomach, her pubic bone under the base of my skull, her thighs on either side of me," the Commander services Offred. "What he is fucking is the lower part of my body. I do not say making love, because this is not what he's doing. Copulating too would be inaccurate, because it would imply two people and only one is involved. Nor does rape cover it. . . . " Despite the text's denial, this passage dramatizes a terrible kind of rape. Because the Handmaid takes on the role of the dutiful child-daughter in the Commander-father's household, the Ceremony, with its degrading oedipal flesh triangle, is presented as a thinly disguised incest drama. In the displaced drama of Janine, the narrative makes explicit reference to the forbidden theme of incest. "So well behaved. . . . More like a daughter to you. . . . One of the family," Offred imagines the Wives saying when the pregnant Janine is "paraded" before them. "Little whores, all of them," is the remark made when Janine has left the room. Although *The Handmaid's Tale* deliberately stages an incest drama, it also defends against

Pioneering psychoanlayst Sigmund Freud poses with his daughter, Sophie, in around 1912. J. Brooks Bouson argues that The Handmaid's Tale *can be read as a reaction to Freud's theory of female development.* © Imagno/Contributor/Getty Images.

it by focusing attention on Offred's involvement in an all "too banal" plot. In her relationship with the Commander she has become the mistress of a man whose wife doesn't understand him.

Consent and Defiance in Gilead

A character that students find both puzzling and troubling, the Commander is figured as both a protector and a persecutor. For although he wants to make Offred's life more bearable, he also affirms the masculinist ideology that subordinates and sexually enslaves women. In Gilead, he claims, women are "protected" so that they "can fulfill their biological destinies in peace." Teresa de Lauretis, in her description of "Freud's story of femininity," remarks that for Freud the "difficult journey of the female child to womanhood . . . leads to the fulfillment of her biological destiny, to reproduction." Freud's notion that "reproduction is 'to some extent independent of women's consent' makes us pause," remarks de Lauretis. "While 'the aim of biology' may be accomplished independently of women's consent, the aim of desire (heterosexual male desire, that is) may not. In other words, women *must either* consent *or* be seduced into consenting to femininity." Focusing on women's "consent" to femininity, *The Handmaid's Tale* reveals that what lies behind the benevolent paternalism of the Commander and the culturally conservative ideal of protected womanhood is a rigid belief in male authority and in the hierarchical arrangement of the sexes. In Gilead, women are stripped of their individual identities and transformed into replaceable objects in a phallocentric economy. Bound in a master-slave relationship, the Handmaids are sexual objects for male consumption.

"How numbed Offred's feelings are," remarks one of my students, "yet (thank God), they finally begin writhing under the surface. Her fear which is so powerful at the beginning gives way to defiance." If *The Handmaid's Tale* concerns itself with the troubling issues of incest and forced sex, it also incorporates a feminist retaliatory speech, which partially contains and masters the female fears it dramatizes. Describing how this tactic works, Offred thinks that "there is something powerful in the whispering of obscenities, about those in power. . . . It's like a spell, of sorts. It deflates them, reduces them to the common denominator where they can be dealt with." Indulging in a form of penis ridicule, Offred likens the Commander's penis to a "stub," an extra "thumb," a "tentacle," a "stalked slug's eye." Attending a Gileadean group wedding, she imagines the impressive-looking Commander, who is officiating, in bed with his Wife and Handmaid. "Fertilizing away like mad" and "pretending to take no pleasure in it," he is "like a rutting salmon," in her view. "When the Lord said be fruitful and multiply, did he mean this man?" And she imagines sex among the Angels and their new brides as "momentous grunts and sweating, damp furry encounters; or, better, ignominious failures, cocks like three-week-old carrots, anguished rumblings upon flesh cold and unresponding as uncooked fish."

Externally compliant, Offred expresses her defiance through her "inner jeering" at the Commander. And yet, despite Offred's cynical inner voice, her anger remains largely censored. Claiming, at one point in her narrative reconstruction of events, that she fantasizes stabbing the Commander when he first asks her to kiss him—"I think about the blood coming out of him, hot as soup, sexual, over my hands"—she subsequently denies this impulse. "In fact I don't think about anything of the kind. I put it in only afterwards. . . . As I said, this is a reconstruction." Although Offred fantasizes killing the Commander, she acts out her killing rage against her male oppressors only in the displaced drama of the state-sanctioned Particicution ceremony. When a man accused of rape is thrown at the mercy of a group of Handmaids, he is mobbed and brutally killed. "There is a bloodlust; I want to tear, gouge, rend," as Offred describes it. On the fringes of her tale there is the partially expressed drama of female rage. But in the film version's rewriting of *The Handmaid's Tale*, as my students and I discuss, Offred's angry fantasy of killing the Commander is, indeed, enacted.

Using and Subverting Romance

If the text's rage is acted out in the film version, the novel, in contrast, intertwines its increasing anger about male oppression, which culminates in the Particicution ceremony, with Offred and Nick's love affair. Predictably, some students take comfort in the novel's invocation of romance, which provides Offred—and readers—a temporary escape from the sexually repressive world of Gilead. But students are also open to my analysis of how the novel both uses and subverts the traditional romance plot and romantic discourse.

Although Offred's love affair with Nick is presented as a form of female opposition to the state, the novel's use of the conventional romance plot may appear, at first glance, to present a culturally conservative message to women readers—namely, that only in a love relationship can a woman reach self-fulfillment. And yet if the narrative recuperates the romance plot, it also interrupts it by having Offred tell two radically different versions of her initial sexual encounter with Nick. The first version is erotic. "His mouth is on me, his hands, I can't wait and he's moving, already, love, it's been so long, I'm alive in my skin, again, arms around him, falling and water softly everywhere, never-ending." Claiming that she invented this version of events, Offred then relates another story, which actively undercuts the erotic discourse of the first description. In a telling role reversal, Nick becomes the sexual object and commodity. When he tells her that he could "just squirt it into a bottle" and she could "pour it in," she thinks that perhaps he wants something from her, "some emotion, some acknowledgment that he too is human, is more than just a seedpod." That Offred subsequently admits that it "didn't happen that way either" points to the narrative's reluctance to commit itself to the romance plot. And if Offred's sexual relationship with Nick is presented as an important act of defiance against the Gilead regime, it is also entrapping. For when Nick becomes Offred's lover, she loses her desire to escape

Gilead. Above all else, she wants to be near Nick; with him she feels she can make some kind of life for herself. "Humanity is so adaptable, my mother would say. Truly amazing, what people can get used to, as long as there are a few compensations."

Because of the novel's troubling descriptions of women's sexual exploitation and degradation, which one student reports touched off her own "feelings of being powerless," it is not surprising that student-readers want Offred "to be saved." But if *The Handmaid's Tale* generates a powerful wish to see Offred rescued, it also intentionally leaves the reader in a state of suspense. For as the Eyes help Offred into the black van, she is uncertain whether she is going to her "end" or a "new beginning," whether she is stepping up "into the darkness within; or else the light." Although Offred's fate is left hanging in the balance at the end of her narrative, the "Historical Notes" section appended to her tale acts out the rescue fantasy generated by the narrative. Speculating on what probably happened to her, Professor Pieixoto, the twenty-second-century historian who transcribes Offred's tapes, comments that while her "ultimate fate" is unknown, the weight of evidence suggests that Nick engineered her escape. And her narrative, he claims, has "a certain reflective quality. . . . It has a whiff of emotion recollected, if not in tranquillity, at least *post facto.*"

A Jarring Conclusion

Because many of my students find the "Historical Notes" both jarring and confusing, I spend some time discussing the content and function of this appended material and also commenting on Atwood's presentation, in the character of her pedantic, misogynistic professor, of a "bad" reader, someone who can decode textual puzzles but remains strangely out of touch with the text he is reading. Suggesting that there are appropriate and inappropriate ways of responding to literary texts in the "Historical Notes," Atwood dramatizes her desire to save her novel from those readers who, like her fictional professor, would treat the text as a verbal artifact to be coldly dissected and ultimately dismissed.

"*Come with me*, the writer is saying to the reader," writes Atwood. "*There is a story I have to tell you, there is something you need to know.*" As Atwood reads and interprets women's lives in *The Handmaid's Tale*, she tells a story she wants her women readers to hear and respond to. A novel that women readers find difficult to dismiss, *The Handmaid's Tale* both involves readers emotionally and forces them to pay heed to Atwood's feminist critique of the gender and power politics that drive masculinist culture.

Controlling Women's Voices
in *The Handmaid's Tale*

David S. Hogsette

David S. Hogsette is a professor of English at the New York Institute of Technology, where he also serves as the writing program coordinator.

In literary theory it is generally accepted that people create their identity—and confirm their basic humanity—through the use of language. For this reason, political regimes, both real and imagined, almost invariably control language, placing strict limits on what can be said by whom and who can learn to read or have access to information and communication technology. Even when the disempowered find a way to speak, their words and voices are often co-opted by the powerful. In the following viewpoint, Hogsette argues that, by including the fictional "Historical Notes" (delivered by an arrogant male professor) at the end of the novel, Atwood provides readers with a perfect example of how not to read such a story. Atwood mocks Pieixoto's pedantic, unimaginative reading of Offred's tale in order to congratulate us for fully and emotionally engaging with the text and thus ensuring that Offred's story—and Atwood's own voice—remains intact.

At first glance, *The Handmaid's Tale* (1985) appears to be a radical divergence from Margaret Atwood's traditional novelistic style. Atwood readers who are accustomed to encountering the mysteriously primordial woods of some Canadian outland as in *Surfacing* (1972), the hectic traffic of crowded downtown sidewalks in such novels as *The Edible*

David S. Hogsette, "Margaret Atwood's Rhetorical Epilogue in *The Handmaid's Tale*: The Reader's Role in Empowering Offred's Speech Act," *Critique: Studies in Contemporary Fiction*, Summer 1997, Vol. 38:4, p. 262. Copyright © 1997, Taylor and Francis Books, Ltd. Reproduced by permission.

Woman (1969) and *Life Before Man* (1979), and escapist realms like Italy in *Lady Oracle* (1976) and the Caribbean in *Bodily Harm* (1981) are witness, instead, to political takeover of some unidentified, futuristic North American province. In *The Handmaid's Tale*, Atwood exchanges her traditional realism for science fiction. But even though she leaves behind her contemporary Canada in order to create a futuristic dystopia, Atwood carries with her the significant issues that characterize her previous novels, short stories, and poetry—issues of self-discovery, self-expression, self-construction, gender discrimination, political oppression, and patriarchal domination. However, Atwood distinguishes *The Handmaid's Tale* from her earlier work not only by writing speculative fiction but also by exploring those important feminist and humanist concerns explicitly in terms of the power dynamics of discourse within social, political, and economic communities. Like the poststructuralist perspectives of Jacques Derrida, Michel Foucault, Judith Butler, and Denise Riley, Atwood suggests that language is never value-neutral. That is, she examines the political, social, and sexual dimensions of discourse, focusing specifically on oppression enforced by institutionalized control of acquiring knowledge and using language and on the self-liberating potential of an individual's act of storytelling. Although several critics have carefully explored the ways in which storytelling serves as the impetus for Offred's self-empowerment, no one has yet recognized the way in which Atwood complicates the political effectiveness of narrative acts by ending her novel with the ironic "Historical Notes" epilogue, an ending that demands a rereading of her novel. Significantly, though, this rhetorically induced rereading does not go unguided, for the epilogue's ironic information provides readers with an example of how not to read Atwood's novel and thereby directs readers toward a proper reading of both the novel and Offred's narrative. . . .

Empowerment Through Language

[Feminist critical] discussions of Offred's narrative help to illuminate the complicated linguistic and political nature of *The Handmaid's Tale*, leading us to a richer feminist understanding about why Atwood presents the reader with the limited perspective of a woman trapped in the oppressive, patriarchal society of the Republic of Gilead. Although those critics effectively analyze the political implications of Offred's story, they do not, however, sufficiently examine the potentially disruptive effect that the "Historical Notes" epilogue poses for their feminist readings. They do, of course, discuss the patriarchal structure of this post-Gilead society and Professor Pieixoto's chauvinistic misreading of Offred's narrative. But they do not consider the political ramifications of Pieixoto's compilation of Offred's text. Such a compilation forces us to ask crucial questions regarding the liberating effect and power of Offred's speaking out. Does Offred break free of her oppressed state, does she write herself back into history, and express her own subjectivity? Or is it ultimately a chauvinistic man who gives Offred her voice, who allows her to speak, who recaptures her voice within his textual authority?

By more carefully analyzing the ramifications of Pieixoto's (mis)reading of Offred's text, I hope to show how Atwood suggests that effective—and affective—reading plays a significant role in the communicative process through which women regain their voice and become social agents. Indeed, Atwood's primary concern in *The Handmaid's Tale* is to examine the political nature of language use. Offred gradually recognizes that she can manipulate language in order to create her own subjectivity, a subjectivity that can enable her to act as a subversive agent against the oppressive reality created by the Republic of Gilead. However, Atwood's epilogue brings into question Offred's political effectiveness, thus (retrospectively) foregrounding a subtextual dimension to Atwood's primary concern. Atwood not only explores the political potential of the user of language, but also suggests that the receivers of language—listeners or readers—must properly interpret the language the political agent uses for language truly to create a self-empowering subjectivity and reality. Through the epilogue, Atwood suggests that not only must women reinscribe their voices and assert their own subjectivity into the political and historical discourse of their society, but those women's audiences must learn how to read those reinscribed voices and properly interpret their subjective meanings. . . .

Identity Is Constructed Through Language

Because Offred's narrative is not teleological [intended to explain the purpose of Offred's journey] it is difficult to trace the exact development of her linguistic awareness. However, we can notice that immediately following the Gilead takeover, Offred begins to realize the existence of a relationship among language, the self, institutions, and power. For example, when Offred first meets Serena Joy, Offred carefully considers how she should respond to Serena's questions. Offred realizes her lowly position and does not wish unduly to magnify her social oppression by having her words misinterpreted as an insult. Offred apparently already understands that language must be interpreted and can therefore be misinterpreted, and that language and institutional power are related. She does not wish to worsen her already lowly social-household status by possibly offending Serena. Offred's awareness of the effects of Serena's possible misinterpretation not only reveals how quickly Offred has learned the power dynamic of oppressor and oppressed but also provides a basis upon which she gradually builds her understanding of the political, social, and humanistic ramifications of language. Her first step toward that realization comes when she ponders the multiplicity of meaning of a single word. For example, as she waits for her dinner one evening, Offred contemplates the various levels of meaning associated with the word "chair":

> I sit in the chair and think about the word chair. It can also
> mean the leader of a meeting. It can also mean a mode of
> execution. It is the first syllable in charity. It is the French
> word for flesh. None of these facts has any connection with
> the others. These are the kinds of litanies I use, to compose
> myself.

Although her contemplation of the complexity of language
calms her mentally, Offred is not yet fully aware of the impact
of her language, as [Linda] Kauffman points out. "But in fact
there is an associative connection [among the different meanings of the word 'chair'], for the leaders of the revolution enforce their power by torturing the flesh of dissenters. Resisters
receive no charity, no mercy; instead, they are executed." But
even though Offred does not yet realize the full political potential of making associative connections between the different meanings of a single word, she is, at least, intellectually
exploring—however aimlessly—the various dimensions of
meaning inherent in language. Most important, however, is
Offred's attempt to "compose" or reconstruct her identity with
those litanies. She directly connects language and identity and
indirectly relates the way in which the social and institutional
dimensions of language play a part in how individuals use
language to construct their own identities. As [Chris] Weedon
observes language is "the place where our sense of ourselves,
our subjectivity, is constructed . . . in ways which are socially
specific." Only by making a connection between the Gilead
power structures and language can Offred use her speech act
to construct a subjectivity that can enable her to serve as an
agent for social and political change.

It is easy for contemporary readers like Kauffman to be
slightly critical of Offred for not noticing the connections between the meanings of the word "chair"; however, we must
not forget that she has lost many of her language skills because of the Republic's information-communication policy
that restricts reading and speaking to only a carefully selected

few. As Offred begins her rediscovery of the intricacies of language, she cannot comprehend all at once its political potential. But she does continue to redevelop her understanding of language, ironically, with inadvertent help from the Commander, one of those "select few." When she secretly visits the Commander in his office, Offred indulges in the forbidden fruit of language, playing Scrabble and reading women's magazines such as *Vogue* and *Mademoiselle*. She actively rebuilds her vocabulary and strengthens her command over the language:

> My tongue felt thick with the effort of spelling. It was like using a language I'd once known but had nearly forgotten . . . It was like trying to walk without crutches, like those phony scenes in old TV movies. You can do it. I know you can. That was the way my mind lurched and stumbled, among the sharp R's and T's, sliding over the ovoid vowels as if on pebbles.

Reclaiming the Power of Words

Initially, Offred does not understand the Commander's motives, suspecting his invitations may involve sexual perversion. Later, she realizes that the Commander himself may not understand his own intentions: "I thought he might be toying, some cat-and-mouse routine, but now I think that his motives and desires weren't obvious even to him. They had not yet reached the level of words." But as the gaming and the reading continue, Offred develops her ability to raise those desires to the "level of words," finally deciding that the Commander longs for a community and emotional sharing that his wife does not provide him. For Offred that is clearly an insult: "That's what I was there for, then. The same old thing. It was too banal to be true". She is a toy, a whim that fills in for the deficiencies of his wife. However, while the Commander satisfies his banal desires, Offred reacquaints herself with language and the language user's ability to create positive and negative images of the self. By gazing at magazines whose articles and fashion layouts construct specific images of womanhood, Offred rediscovers the ability of an individual and a society to use language (textual and iconographic) to (re)construct self-images. The Commander's office, a major intelligence center for the Republic of Gilead, is ironically a training ground for a growing dissenting voice. Offred redevelops her control of language, thus enabling her to recreate and ultimately assert her own subjectivity. . . .

Most important for Offred's growing awareness of the liberating power of language is her discovery of the Latin sentence Nolite te bastardes carborundorum [don't let the bastards grind you down] inscribed in her closet by her predecessor. As [Michelle] LaCombe aptly notes, "In the absence of genuine faith, the writing on the closet floor becomes the focus of buried hope and itself appears as an act of charity by the previous female tenant." Equally important, Offred realizes that language can be used as a force of resistance. Those scribblings left by a desperate Handmaid serve as words of encouragement and suggest that defiance is possible: "It pleases me to know that her taboo message made it through, to at least one person, washed itself up on the wall of my cupboard, was opened and read by me. Sometimes I repeat the words to myself. They give me a small joy." Those words grant Offred the faith that her own narrative may be uncovered by some future-reader. Like the writer of that Latin sentence, Offred intends her own text for whoever comes next, and that text will create or materialize Offred's reality for that intended "whoever." Offred learns that language, as Weedon explains, is a mode of resistance: "Once language is understood in terms of competing discourses, competing ways of giving meaning to the world, which imply differences in the organization of social power, then language becomes an important site of political struggle." . . .

Co-opting Others' Voices

In the epilogue, we learn that Professor James Pieixoto and Professor Wade of the University of Cambridge have uncovered and reassembled Offred's narrative. The clearly misogynistic Pieixoto, who introduces his lecture with several sexist jokes, puns, and witticisms engages in textual interpretation much like that of Gilead's ruling elite. LaCombe explains the interpretive strategies of that theocratically totalitarian government:

> ... the language of Gilead is the phallocentric word made flesh, the vehicle of a totalitarian state based upon literal interpretation of the Bible, at least as it is to be understood by the masses. The uses of such literalmindedness are emphasized by the falsification of Biblical texts and their eventual merger with the canon.

In other words, the men of Gilead appropriate the text of the Bible to fit their political, social, and sexual goals. In the Red Center, for example, the Aunts play a tape of a man reading the Beatitudes during the Handmaids' lunch. Of one of the Beatitudes, Offred comments, "I knew they made that up, I knew it was wrong, and they left things out, too, but there was no way of checking." The Bible—a text concerned with freedom from sin, freedom from death, and hope of salvation—is used, as it has been throughout the history of Western civilization, to subjugate and oppress. Similarly, Offred's text—a text of hope that signifies her empowerment—becomes appropriated by the literal-minded Pieixoto. Offred's voice, captured on tape, is inscribed by the interpretive acts of a man.

Having finished his lecture on the historical nature of Offred's text, Pieixoto asks his audience, "Are there any questions?" Indeed, there are many questions, but the most troubling for me is the following critical issue: how heroic is Offred's act of rediscovering and transmitting her voice when we consider that her text is exposed to (and composed by) a

Natasha Richardson as Offred in the 1990 film adaptation of The Handmaid's Tale. © Photos 12/Alamy.

chauvinistically focused light? For, indeed, if Offred's narrative is reassembled and appropriated by the chauvinistic Pieixoto as the epilogue suggests, then Offred's development into a social agent through speaking out is retrospectively drawn into question, if not completely undermined. In other words, can we consider Offred's text self-liberating if it is Pieixoto who defragments the narrative by imposing his own phallocentric order onto her text? . . .

Reappraising Offred's Tale

In the case of *The Handmaid's Tale*, the meaning a reader makes of Offred's narrative must be retrospectively influenced by the information provided in the epilogue. Therefore, after meeting the chauvinistic professor of the epilogue who, as the reader learns, has uncovered Offred's tapes and has admittedly assembled (rewritten, recreated) Offred's text somewhat arbitrarily, or at least in an order about which he is not totally confident, the reader must consider how to interpret this fact that Offred's text has been appropriated by a male. Could it be that Offred has not reclaimed her voice at all? It appears that Pieixoto reinscribes her text, thus trapping her within his textual authority, his sense of history, and his vision of how her life should be pieced together and presented. A man grants her the chance to speak and orders the way in which her words will be received. Offred becomes Ofjames.

But is this an appropriate retroactive reading of Atwood's novel? Is Atwood's point that women's words will forever be appropriated and thus obscured and oppressed by male voices? The ironic intent of the epilogue suggests the answer to these questions is no. Pieixoto is characterized as valuing scientific objectivity and is thus interested only in accurately transcribing Offred's narrative. He views her text as a cultural artifact, ultimately judging her narrative in terms of historical accuracy. He dares not call what he discovered a document because it does not include factual data, such as historical dates and substantive names or a few pages from her Commander's computer. The irony here reveals that Pieixoto's attempt at being objective is itself a subjective act. His academic pursuit of Offred's "true" past is informed by intellectual expectations as to what constitutes a "document" and what forms of information best represent history. In the epilogue, Atwood uses irony to assert that historical representation is itself a fiction and that the historian can never achieve objective distance from his or her narrative subject. Therefore, the historian has an obligation to recognize his or her biases, political stances, and cultural and social expectations and then to acknowledge those factors when transcribing history. Because Pieixoto does not recognize the constructed nature of his (narrative) historical account of Offred's narrative, he is blinded by his intellectualizing and fails to comprehend Offred's isolation, her subjugation, and the heroic significance of the risk she took in attempting to record her thoughts and feelings. Instead, he transcribes Offred's tapes, word for word, ordering the narrative according to scholarly principles of logic and coherence. He creates textual gaps and adds emphasis to words and phrases in an effort to recapture Offred's tone and her occasional pauses. However, Pieixoto fails to understand those textual gaps and inflections. He becomes so engaged in what he considers accurate transcription that he misinterprets Offred's text.

The irony of the epilogue not only points out Pieixoto's interpretive shortcomings, but it also serves as a negative directive on how to read Offred's narrative. In other words, Pieixoto's compilation and description of Offred's text is an illustration of how not to read her text. Instead of intellectually objectifying Offred's voice, thus stripping it of its social and political efficacy, we should try to think the way Offred thinks and to empathize with her human condition. We must recognize that Offred's text is far from being incomplete or insignificant historically, mere "crumbs the Goddess of History has deigned to vouchsafe us." And we must not dismiss her narrative as if it were naive and nostalgic drivel, characterized by Romantic imaginative and emotional embellishment: "It has a whiff of emotion recollected, if not in tranquillity, at least post facto." Offred's narrative not only relays the political, social, and human devastation of her dystopian community, but it also serves as Atwood's cautionary tale to her contemporary audience. Atwood uses the epilogue in order to instruct her readers how to construct themselves as the audience of her contemporary novel and of Offred's dystopian narrative. . . .

Freeing Offred from Her Male Interpreters

Obviously, it is difficult to identify and adopt the appropriate critical stance of the different audiences of Atwood's speculative novel. However, with the "Historical Notes" chapter Atwood presents a scenario of improper reading in order to teach her readers how to construct themselves as the contemporary audience of her novel and the sympathetic audience of Offred's narrative. The flesh-and-blood reader must realize that:

> Professor Pieixoto does not know how to describe the document as a genre; in terms of gender, he is condescending, ascribing the aleatory [random] construction of the discourse, its lack of style, to the poor education of North American females in the 1980s, and apologizing for the quality of Offred's mind. (Kauffman)

The professor completely misreads Offred's text. He does not understand her perspective; nor does he make any effort to join the audience of her autobiography. Even though *The Handmaid's Tale* is a speculative or science fiction novel, the flesh-and-blood audience of this novel must attempt a reading dynamic appropriate for more "realistic" works of fiction. We see that in the epilogue, Pieixoto, a fictitious reader of a fictitious autobiography, does not become a member of Offred's audience. The epilogue enables Atwood to reinforce a proper reading of her novel, a reading that involves avoiding Pieixoto's blind scholarly reading pattern and extending beyond our subjective frames of reference, thus simultaneously becoming a member of Atwood's and Offred's respective audiences.

In actively joining Offred's audience, the reader discovers what Pieixoto covers up. The telling of this narrative is the ultimate culmination of her own particular feminist bildungsroman [a story of personal growth], that is, Offred matures into political awareness and shares with her audience the forbidden fruit of her knowledge. Before the Republic of Gilead's oppressive regime came to power, Offred lived a life of political complacency. Even though her mother was a radical feminist, Offred turned away from politics:

> Now, Mother, I would say. Let's not get into an argument about nothing. Nothing, she'd say bitterly. You call it nothing. You don't understand, do you. You don't understand at all what I'm talking about.

Offred did not care about politics and how societal events could directly affect her personal life. Through active ignoring, through exercising her freedom not to care, Offred did not notice the gradual encroachment of the subjugating power of Gilead.

Even as she narrates her story, Offred contemplates the futility of speaking out. She considers withdrawing into her self and dismissing any responsibility she may feel toward contributing to the cause of liberating women:

> I don't have to tell it [her story]. I don't have to tell anything, to myself or to anyone else. I could just sit here, peacefully. I could withdraw. It's possible to go so far in, so far down and back, they could never get you out.

> *Nolite te bastardes carborundorum.* Fat lot of good it did her.

> Why fight?

> That will never do.

The textual gap between "Why fight?" and "That will never do" is an important clue to Offred's personal political development. Interestingly, though, it is Pieixoto who represents that gap. Again, the question must be asked, is it Pieixoto who grants Offred her voice? Is Pieixoto aware of the significance of such a break in the text and does he thus create the meaning in Offred's stead? The answer to those questions is clearly no. Pieixoto is concerned only with accurately transcribing Offred's narrative. He places the textual gap to indicate a pause in Offred's speech, but his purely scholarly interests blind him to the significance of the break. The reader who constructs himself or herself as Atwood's and Offred's respective audiences realizes the meaning: the textual gap demarks a pause in Offred's oration, a pause where she considers the ramifications of her selfishness and ultimately decides to contribute to the resistance in the best way she knows how. Furthermore, she comes to a better understanding of the phrase "Nolite te bastardes carborundorum." Before that message from Offred's predecessor can mean or signify, Offred must learn how to translate it and apply it to her life. She realizes that she can and must resist Gilead by leaving a narrative account of her experiences so as, in the very least, to provide spiritual and moral support to anyone who encounters her tale in the same way her predecessor's message aided her. Moreover, when read retrospectively in light of Pieixoto's misreading of Offred's narrative, her growing understanding of that message serves as an analogue to our self-construction as readers: just as Offred must properly construct herself in order to understand the scribbled message properly, we must construct ourselves as the audience of Atwood's novel and Offred's tale so that we may correctly understand and appreciate Atwood's political message and Offred's political activism.

The Importance of the Audience

However, the act of writing or speaking, though valiant in its own right, is not enough. Weedon makes an important observation: "The site of this battle for power is the subjectivity of the individual and it is a battle in which the individual is an active but not sovereign protagonist." Indeed, the subjective speaker is not sovereign. As Atwood's epilogue suggests, the political voice of women that breaks from its earlier silenced state can be appropriated by men, thus threatening women again with silence. Women's voices must not only be expressed, but must also be received. Those voices need an audience. But that audience must be willing to empathize with the speaker and must be careful not to off-read, so to speak, that speaker's voice. Offred attempts to mandate the audience's empathy by creating her own audience: "Because I am telling you this story I will your existence. I tell, therefore you are." Her efforts, however, are not fully successful, for Pieixoto ignores or, at least, is blind to Offred's wishes. The individual reader, then, must actively construct himself or herself as the specific audience that Offred wills into being. With the "Historical Notes" epilogue serving as an explicit directive on how not to read Offred's narrative, the actual reader discovers that he or she must be a patient, sympathetic, and understanding audience of not only Offred's story but also Atwood's novel. Only then will the reader recognize Offred's heroic rediscovery of her voice and understand Atwood's political vision: the power of language involves two agents—a performer and an audience. Through the dynamic dialectic occurring between those two agents, a woman's voice can be truly heard.

Consequently, Atwood extends the theory of constructionism beyond the writer-speaker, applying it directly to readers as well. She suggests that in addition to the writer-speaker's learning how to construct herself in relation to certain political, social, and economic discourses through an active manipulation of language, readers must also learn how to construct themselves in a particular way so as to understand the writer-speaker's self-construction. Because all identities are constructions, readers, when attempting to join Offred's audience, must engage in the very same act of self-construction as she does. The act of reading, much like the act of writing-speaking, thus becomes a fundamental component of the writer's process of subjectivity and political empowerment. In other words, writing as a political act is incomplete without the act of reading. And because reading is a dynamic emotional and intellectual dialectic occurring between the reader and the author's text (a dialectic whose synthesis produces the politicized and politicizing work), self-liberation and political empowerment never occur in isolation, but must always involve a community consisting of author agent(s) and audience agent(s), even if that community is composed simply of a single individual from both agent groups.

Women Oppress Women in Atwood's Novel

Tara J. Johnson

Tara J. Johnson studied and taught literary theory at Ball State University, specifically focusing on Jewish and feminist studies.

In the following viewpoint, Johnson demonstrates that, as has been the case throughout history, the oppressed minority in Gilead—in other words, women—is controlled by a group drawn from its own ranks—in this case, the Aunts. Although it is hard to establish whether or not the Aunts actually have more power in Gilead than the Commanders, the author argues that it is certainly the case that in their role controlling the female population, the Aunts are far more vital than any Commander to ensuring the continuation of the Republic.

Many scholars, both male and female alike, dismiss the Aunts in Margaret Atwood's *The Handmaid's Tale* as having a token power granted to them by the Commanders in Gilead. In fact, the males in positions of Commanders are given full responsibility for creating and maintaining the Gileadan theocracy many years after the dissolution of Gilead in the novel's blatantly satiric epilogue. Lee Briscoe Thompson in her book *Scarlet Letters: Margaret Atwood's "The Handmaid's Tale"* believes that lecturer Professor James Darcy Pieixoto's "real interest" is in "the male power elite of Gilead" which means that he would dismiss any female involvement. Karen Stein in her article "Margaret Atwood's Modest Proposal: *The Handmaid's Tale*" describes the dystopic Gilead in this manner: "In the guise of a re-population program, Gilead reads the biblical text literally and makes it the basis for the state-sanctioned rape, the impregnation ceremony the handmaids must undergo each month." The society is obviously founded upon principles that negate the rights of women, which would lead readers to believe that no woman, let alone a group of women, could have the type and the strength of the power of the Commanders. Critics such as Roberta Rubenstein in her article "Nature and Nurture in Dystopia: *The Handmaid's Tale*" believe that the Aunts only "retain power in the puritanical state through their role as indoctrinators of the handmaids." This paper would argue that the Aunts were created by Atwood and portrayed in such a manner as to suggest that they have as much if not more power as the Commanders have.

Oppressing Women with Women

Atwood has a history of placing powerful females in her novels who use their power against other females, and the Aunts in *The Handmaid's Tale* are a clear type of this feminine power. The Aunts fall into the long tradition of females with power in Atwood's novels. *Cat's Eye*, Atwood's novel immediately following *The Handmaid's Tale*, continues this tradition. While most of the criticism concerning *Cat's Eye* is about Elaine Risley's ability to find her own power (after being tortured by her childhood friend), Cordelia and her treatment of Elaine are reminiscent of the Aunts and their treatment of females, and the Handmaids in particular. According to J. Brooks Bouson, "*The Handmaid's Tale* anticipates *Cat's Eye*'s dramatization of the female-directed oppression of women (which begins during the girlhood socialization process) and it describes the brutal reeducation of the Handmaids, who are coerced by the Aunts to forego the ideology of women's liberation and to revert to the 'traditional' values of a male-dominated system."

Atwood intentionally created the Aunts as powerful females in a dystopia. In a radio conversation with fellow writer Victor-Levy Beaulieu, she said that the character of Aunt Lydia "is based on the history of imperialisms. For example, the British in India raised an army of Indians to control the rest of the Indians . . . So, if you want to control women, you have to grant some women a tiny bit more power so that they'll control the others." In a BBC World Book Club radio program last year [2003], Margaret Atwood stated: "I think the Aunts [in *The Handmaid's Tale*] have quite a bit of power . . . Naturally, they would have to answer to a top level of men." And during Professor Pieixoto's examination of the Gileadan theocracy in the novel's epilogue, he clearly notes Atwood's observation:

> Judd—according to the Limkin material—was of the opinion from the outset that the best and most cost-effective way to control women . . . was through women themselves. For this there were many historical precedents; in fact, no empire imposed by force or otherwise has ever been without this feature: control of the indigenous members by their own group.

The Aunts Perpetuate Gilead

By taking this power offered to them, the Aunts were therefore able to "escape redundancy, and consequent shipment to the infamous Colonies, which were composed of portable populations used mainly as expendable toxic-cleanup squads, though if lucky could be assigned to less hazardous tasks, such as cotton picking and fruit harvesting." According to Thompson, it is "the pleasures of power" that "seal the deal" along with the "small perks" and "personal security." Thompson claims the Aunts to be "a classic depiction of Victim Position #1 as described in Atwood's analysis of victimhood in her literary study *Survival*." While the Aunts may be victims of a male hierarchy, they certainly choose to utilize the power that they have over other women.

Linda Myrsiades in her article "Law, Medicine, and the Sex Slave in Margaret Atwood's *The Handmaid's Tale*" simply categorizes the Aunts as "a class of women assigned to educate the handmaids to their roles as surrogates." David Coad in his article "Hymens, Lips and Masks: The Veil in Margaret Atwood's *The Handmaid's Tale*" limits the role of the Aunts by saying that they are merely "sadistic propagandists." It could be argued, however, that the Aunts are responsible for sustaining the rituals of the Gileadan society, and not only the training of the Handmaids at the Rachel and Leah Reeducation Center. When Janine, or Ofwarren, is ready to give birth, Aunt Elizabeth plays an integral part in the birthing process for both Janine and the Commander's wife. At the assembly of the Handmaids, Aunt Lydia directs both the Salvaging and the Particicution ceremonies. Lucy M. Freibert in her article "Control and Creativity: The Politics of Risk in Margaret Atwood's *The Handmaid's Tale*" describes both ceremonies in this manner: "At the hangings each Handmaid must touch the rope in assent to the murders. At Particicutions the Handmaids ritually dismember any man accused of rape. The Aunts supply the rhetoric that arouses the women to savagery." The Aunts are also responsible for directing the females who are not Handmaids. When Offred goes with the Commander to the club, which serves as a brothel for the Commanders, she is surprised to see that an Aunt is responsible for regulating the behavior of her friend Moira and the other prostitutes. The Aunt determines when the prostitutes take their breaks and for how long the breaks are. The Aunt also determines whether they need to lose weight in their positions and will punish them if they are overweight. A comparison of the Aunts' responsibility and the Commanders' responsibility shows that the Commanders are in charge of much lighter duties. A Commander officiates the arranged marriages service. The Commander is responsible for reading Bible passages to his household. The Commander is also responsible for impregnating the Handmaid in order to continue Gilead. It is clear that the Aunts have more responsibilities in the Gileadan theocracy than merely educating women for service as Handmaids.

Aunts More Powerful than Wives

Most scholarly criticism focuses on the Aunts' responsibility for maintaining the Rachel and Leah Reeducation Center. According to Barbara Hill Rigney in her book *Margaret Atwood*, "the control agency in this novel is, not the commanders, but the 'Aunts', who run their re-education centres with cattle prods, torture techniques, and brain washing slogans." The Aunts have very clear goals that they want to accomplish with their training of the Handmaids. The first is to delete the women from history: "All official records of the handmaids would have been destroyed upon their entry into the Rachel and Leah Re-education Center." The second goal is to teach women how to betray other women. [As explained by Thompson,] Offred learns from the Aunts that "the only storytellings permitted or rewarded are informing on others or testifying against oneself." The Handmaids learn that their behavior will be reported if it is thought to undermine the Gileadan regime. According to the Aunts, "friendships were suspicious." Aunt Lydia wants Janine to listen to the other Handmaids and tell her if anyone had helped Moira to escape. Ironically, after all of Janine's efforts to appease the Aunts, she has a mental breakdown when her baby is deemed a Shredder rather than a Keeper. The Aunts' final goal is to teach the Handmaids that rape is acceptable. They are able to utilize Janine's gang rape to further this lesson as they wear her down and make her realize that her gang rape was her fault. The other Handmaids learn how to call Janine a crybaby and jeer at her when she cries and is upset. Janine's gang rape story is a pivotal element in teaching the Handmaids that ritualistic rape at the hands of their Commanders will not only be tolerated but also encouraged. Eleonora Rao in her book *Strategies for Identity: The Fiction of Margaret Atwood* notes that Moira is one female who "survives intact the programme of conditioning into the acceptance of female guilt and evil imposed on the handmaids at the Centre." The Aunts are not only training the Handmaids, they are creating women who will not only submit to their Commanders but also further the goals of the Gileadan theocracy.

A clear indication that the Aunts have a more elevated status than other females in Gilead, including the wives, is the power that they hold above other females. Thompson agrees with me about this, describing the Aunts as "a paramilitary cadre in charge of indoctrinating Handmaids and enforcing female (even Wifely) obedience to the new rules." Thompson goes on to say that "the Aunts wear army khaki without veils, befitting their quasi-military role, and reminiscent of the fascistic Brownshirts of World War II (not to mention the no less fascist childhood Brownie troop uniforms of other Atwood fiction!)." Thompson states that the other females are not allowed to wear the "Aunt khaki since they have no administrative powers." Included in the Aunts' administrative powers is the use of violence and other methods to fight resistance from other females. At the Rachel and Leah Reeducation Center, the Aunts have the power to put "some kind of pill or drug" in the food to keep the Handmaids disoriented so that they won't resist in the beginning. Offred notes that when Moira arrives at the Center she has a bruise on her left cheek. When Dolores, a Handmaid in training, wets the floor because she isn't allowed to go to the bathroom, the Aunts haul her away and the Handmaids listen to her moan all night after she returns. For Moira's first attempt at escaping from the Center, she is beaten with steel cables on both of her feet and the other Handmaids have to carry her because she can't walk. The Aunts are very honest about their willingness to use violence to accomplish their goals: "Remember. For our purposes your feet and your hands are not essential." The Aunts' use of violence is important because even the Wives are not allowed to use force to abuse or punish the Handmaids. Another power that the Aunts have in comparison to the other female characters is the permission to publicly read and write. No woman is allowed to read and write in Gileadan society. On the night of the Handmaid's impregnation Ceremony, the Commander unlocks the drawer that holds the Bible and reads aloud to the women in his household. Only the Commanders and the Aunts are allowed to read and write.

The Commanders Undermine Gilead

Central to understanding the power of the Aunts is Moira's successful escape in the guise of an Aunt from the Rachel and Leah Reeducation Center and future servitude as a Handmaid. Moira forcibly exchanges clothing with an Aunt and instantly becomes a respectable, powerful woman in Gileadan society. Moira had previously attempted to use her own power and wit by faking the symptoms of scurvy and was unable to escape from the Center. Wearing Aunt Elizabeth's clothing, Moira walks out of the Center and past the barricades set up to prevent women from leaving Gilead. Moira doesn't have to explain the nature of her business to any of the male security personnel. She does end up at the Commanders' club under the watchful eye of an Aunt, but she isn't executed nor is she banished to an Unwoman colony. As Moira explains to Offred when they find each other at the club, "I couldn't believe how easy it was to get out of the Center. In that brown outfit I just walked right through. I kept on going as if I knew where I was heading, till I was out of sight. I didn't have any great plan; it wasn't an organized thing, like they thought. . . ." Even Moira and Offred are surprised that Aunts are respected in the Gileadan theocracy.

The Commanders' behavior is more suggestive of freedom for women than the Aunts' behavior. Sema Kormali in her article "Feminist Science Fiction: The Alternative Worlds of Piercy, Elgin and Atwood" states that "it is the Aunts, as best exemplified by Aunt Lydia, who are probably the most guilty of enforcing this patriarchal/totalitarian rule on the members of their own sex." Furthermore, Karen Stein in her book *Mar-*

garet Atwood Revisited states that the role of Aunt Lydia [and the other Aunts] is to control "women's appetites for freedom and knowledge, slimming down their minds and behaviors to be acceptable to Gilead's social standards." When Offred goes with the Commander to the club, she views her and the Commander's behavior as ". . . flaunting, such a sneer at the Aunts, so sinful, so free." The Commander allows Offred rights that the Gileadan regime and the Aunts deny her. In his study, the Commander shares women's magazines such as *Vogue* and novels with her. Offred is able to write out words while she is playing Scrabble with the Commander. Furthermore, Offred says "the Commander was patient when I hesitated, or asked him for a correct spelling." This behavior of the Commander's demonstrates his willingness for her to possibly relearn what she has forgotten and to increase her own vocabulary. Another way that he helps her is by explaining what the saying "*Nolite te bastardes carborundorum*" [don't let the bastards grind you down] inscribed on her bedroom floor means. When Serena Joy later reprimands Offred for spending intimate time with her husband, she alludes to the fact that the Commander engaged in similar activities with the former Handmaid in their household. This admission of Serena's confirms Offred's suspicion that she is not the only Handmaid to have been inside the Commander's study to learn what "*Nolite te bastardes carborundorum*" means.

Aunts Have More Power than Commanders

While the Commanders are undermining the Gileadan theocracy with their behavior, the Aunts are promoting the future of Gilead. The Aunts consider the group of women that Offred is a part of to be the "transitional generation. It is the hardest for you. . . . For the ones who come after you, it will be easier." The Aunts tell the Handmaids that the next generation "will accept their duties with willing hearts. . . . Because they won't want what they can't have." The Aunts have a greater capacity for imagining what the future will be like for women in Gilead: "what we're aiming for is a spirit of camaraderie among women." Bouson finds this aim "ironic" because the Aunts "uphold the male supremist power structure of Gilead with its hierarchical arrangement of the sexes, and they play an active role in the state's sexual enslavement of the Handmaids." When the Commander takes Offred to the club, he makes it very clear that the club was created so that "it's like walking into the past." The costumes that Offred and the other women wear at the club are reminiscent of the time before Gilead. Even Offred is shocked: "such cloth—feathers, mauve, pink." And when they arrive, the Commander announces proudly to her that there are "no nicotine-and-alcohol taboos here!" Offred observes that the Commander is "in the courtly phase" like past relations between men and women. Not only has the Commander kissed Offred on her mouth, which is a forbidden act between a Commander and a Handmaid, but also at the club he takes her hand "and kisses it, on the palm." As if they were two teenagers learning the rules of love at a high school dance, at the club the Commander surprises Offred with a room key: "I thought you might enjoy it for a change."

Corel Ann Howells observes that in *The Handmaid's Tale* "individual freedom of choice has been outlawed and everyone has been drafted into the service of the state, classified according to prescribed roles: Commanders, Wives, Aunts, Handmaids, Eyes, down to Guardians and Econowives." What stands out in her observation is how she has used the word "everyone," which suggests that the Commanders do not have power over the Aunts. In contradistinction, Freibert refuses to acknowledge that the Aunts have any type of power or knowledge in Gilead's society. She places the Commanders, Eyes, Angels, and Guardians in a military hierarchy and only points out that "at the Rachel and Leah Center, the Aunts use electric cattle prods to keep the Handmaids in line." Freibert's hierarchy of power is refuted by Atwood's own skillful portrayal of exactly how involved the Aunts were with the design of the Gileadan society in a conversation between Moira and Offred. Moira explains to Offred: "What I didn't know of course was that in those early days the Aunts and even the [Reeducation] Center were hardly common knowledge. It was all secret at first, behind barbed wire. There might have been objections to what they were doing, even then. So, although people had seen the odd Aunt around, they weren't really aware of what they were for." The Aunts are part of the long tradition of powerful females in Atwood's fiction and *The Handmaid's Tale* provides much evidence to support this claim. Atwood portrays the Aunts in such a manner as to suggest that they have as much if not more power as the males in positions of Commanders in *The Handmaid's Tale*.

Contemporary
Perspectives on
Women's Issues

Opponents of Gay Marriage Seek to Restrict Sexual and Marital Freedom for All

Linda Hirshman

Linda Hirshman is a former philosophy professor and the author of Get to Work: A Manifesto for Women in the World.

The California Marriage Protection Act—better known as Proposition 8—was a ballot measure passed in 2008, amending the California Constitution to indicate that "only marriage between a man and a woman is valid or recognized in California." Subsequent court cases have tested the federal constitutionality of this amendment but have been inconclusive. As of early 2011, the US circuit court had ruled Proposition 8 unconstitutional but had also suspended that ruling pending appeal. In the following viewpoint, Hirshman examines one argument made in court by proponents of Proposition 8, who claim that the amendment was intended to "reinstitutionalize" marriage as a union dedicated to raising and protecting natural-born children—an idea that goes directly counter to a decades-long trend of loosening attitudes toward sexual and personal relationships, a key component of the women's rights movement.

The gay-marriage trial, which just closed [in January 2010] in San Francisco, scared me to death. I haven't been this nervous since reading *The Handmaid's Tale*, Margaret Atwood's fantasy of an America ruled by sexual fundamentalists who took over after a plague of infertility threatened the national survival. The protagonist, the Handmaid, had been a gainfully employed and liberated woman, who married for love and

Supporters and opponents of California's controversial Proposition 8, which banned homosexual couples from marrying, rally outside of the state's Supreme Court Building on March 5, 2009. © David Paul Morris/Stringer/Getty Images.

used birth control to separate sex from reproduction. After the revolution she was enslaved as a childbearer in a lifelong intact family belonging to a Commander of the new society, an embodied womb, in her own words. Although it seems a long way from resisting gay marriage to Atwood's sexual totalitarianism, it turns out resisting gay marriage is just the most visible part of the defendants' program to enforce through law the ideal of lifelong, reproductive Christian monogamy. It's not just gay men and lesbians who transgress. Anyone who isn't marrying in order to procreate and anyone who's procreating outside of marriage is potentially out of bounds.

Childbearing in the Definition of Marriage

The most chilling moment came when gay marriage opponents' witness David Blankenhorn finished describing how the sexual revolution had already weakened marriage, a relationship designed to channel heterosexual reproduction into a biological family that will take good care of the children sex produces. Selfish, happiness-seeking adults and the resulting divorces and out-of-wedlock childbirths had eaten away at the support for marriage, he continued, a process he calls "deinstitutionalization." "By the way," he said, glaring out at the roomful of mostly straight lawyers and media (including this reporter), "it was the heterosexuals who deinstitutionalized marriage. Marriage was weakened long before the movement for same-sex marriage."

You talkin' to *me?* Other commentators have noticed that the same-sex marriage opponents' definition of sex and marriage would make a bunch of straight relationships a little dicey. But once the witnesses and lawyers for the opponents started describing their agenda, things got a lot worse fast. Early on, the defendants' lawyers revealed that they were only concerned about marriage, because children did better if they were raised in married, two-parent families. Not just any two-parent families, but their biological families. "Intact biological families," attorney David Thompson reminded the court, were the gold standard the defendants were trying to advance. So any comparison between children raised by same-sex couples and heterosexual offspring is tainted, because the heterosexual control group includes the dreaded adoptive parents. To say nothing of the worst-case scenario: Singles raising children on their own.

The other shoe dropped Wednesday [January 23, 2010], when Blankenhorn testified that the law could be used to ban or discourage family forms less than ideal for children. After all, he opined, polygamy was banned in part because it was considered bad for children. Following this logic, divorce, too, could be banned, for its role in changing ideal biological intact families into either singles or stepfamilies; adultery could be recriminalized for the role it plays in triggering divorce. Turns out Blankenhorn was part of a study that recommended single mothers give up their babies for adoption—even adoptive families being considered better than single ones. In this vision, the married couple is essentially bound for life by their duties to their children.

An Uncanny Echo of Atwood's Novel

In an uncanny echo of the Atwood novel, early in the trial, the defendants' lawyer David Thompson suggested that deinstitutionalizing marriage was linked to alarmingly low fertility rates. Not surprisingly, then, Blankenhorn resisted any suggestion that there could be marriages that don't involve sex. (In a wicked coincidence, the judge in the case, Vaughn Walker, had presided over a wedding for two presumably non-reproducing octogenarians right before the trial started.) Even a prisoner who doesn't get conjugal privileges will "consummate" the marriage "when he gets out," the witness testified. This concept of marriage cast doubt on the unions of the numerous couples who tell pollsters they never get any. Conversely, it also seems to justify marital rape—a legal doctrine that happily mostly ended when the feminist movement came along. If marriage means sex, how can a wife resist?

Free love; free people. There are many ways that freedom was lost in Atwood's terrible vision: Abortionists were murdered by ravening crowds in stadiums, and the Handmaids forbidden to read. But the consistent and original theme of the work is that freedom to choose whether and why to have sex is a crucial part of meaningful freedom. The Handmaid only finds liberation when she steals out of her room to bed the chauffeur. Atwood writes a pretty good sex scene, but the freedom in the act is vastly sexier than the sex is.

It's funny to think that asking to be allowed to marry would serve the interest of sexual freedom. But in revealing the profoundly repressive sexual agenda of the gay marriage opponents, the trial revealed for the 1,000th time how no one's freedom is safe when anyone's freedom is in peril.

The Surrogacy Market in India Exploits Vulnerable Women

Amana Fontanella-Khan

Amana Fontanella-Khan lives in Mumbai, India, and frequently contributes to the Christian Science Monitor, *the* Hindustan Times, *and* CNN.com.

Amidst the booming surrogacy industry in India, vulnerable women find themselves manipulated into pregnancy and virtually trapped in "surrogacy homes," with little or no legal way to extricate themselves. In the following viewpoint, Fontanella-Khan argues that as India leaps from a developing country to a world-class economic powerhouse, the nation is becoming increasingly divided between those living in a modern, progressive, and urban India of the future and those who continue to eke out their living in the rural, underdeveloped India of the past.

You can outsource just about any work to India these days, including making babies. Reproductive tourism in India is now a half-a-billion-dollar-a-year industry, with surrogacy services offered in 350 clinics across the country since it was legalized in 2002. The primary appeal of India is that it is cheap, hardly regulated, and relatively safe. Surrogacy can cost up to $100,000 in the United States, while many Indian clinics charge $22,000 or less. Very few questions are asked. Same-sex couples, single parents and even busy women who just don't have time to give birth are welcomed by doctors. As a bonus, many Indians speak English and Indian surrogate mothers are less likely to use illegal drugs. Plus medical standards in private hospitals are very high (not all good Indian doctors left in the brain drain).

Surrogacy Gone Awry

Some describe this as a win-win situation. The doctors get clients, the childless get children and the surrogates get much-needed money. But some media horror stories have challenged this happy vision. In 2007 the Japanese couple Ikufumi and Yuki Yamada came to visit India's "Surrogacy Queen," Dr. Nayna Patel, founder of the Akanksha Infertility Clinic. A donor egg and surrogate mother was found and the embryo was implanted in the surrogate's womb. Before the child was born, however, the Yamadas divorced and Mrs. Yamada no longer wanted the child, which was not biologically hers. Mr. Yamada wanted the baby but could not adopt it due to an Indian colonial-era law that forbids single men from adopting girls. The absence of regulation meant that Baby Manji became India's first "surrogate orphan" until the father was finally able to adopt her several months [later], after the Supreme Court intervened. Other cases like the Japanese one have followed, involving Israeli, French, and German citizens.

The most shocking stories, however, concern the surrogate mothers. The surrogates, many of whom are cooped up in "surrogacy homes" away from their families for the duration of the pregnancy, are often in dire financial straits. One woman told a journalist that with a $4,000 debt and an alcoholic husband, she had first considered selling a kidney to get herself out of debt, but decided that the $7,000 surrogacy fee was the better option. In another disturbing case, an upper-class Indian woman hired a surrogate to carry her child and invited her to live in her home during the pregnancy. The client accused the surrogate mother of stealing and not only kicked her out of the house but coolly informed her that she didn't want her services anymore and that she should terminate the pregnancy. Surrogates get paid only on delivery of the baby, so this kind of situation is economically devastating for a surrogate. It can also severely compromise the ethical and religious beliefs of surrogates who may not wish to undergo an abortion.

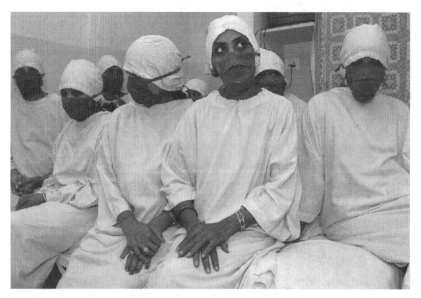

A group of surrogate mothers at India's Kaival Hospital on February 28, 2006. Amana Fontanella-Khan argues that surrogates, who often come from poor and uneducated backgrounds, are exploited by wealthy Western countries. © AP Photo/Ajit Solanki.

Two Indias, One Exploiting the Other

Last year [2009], the government began looking to regulate the industry. An Assisted Reproductive Technology Bill is up for discussion in the next parliamentary session, causing renewed interest in the ethical issues. "Surrogacy—Exploiting the Poor?" was one theme of a very popular, Oprah Winfrey-esque talk show on India's NDTV channel. One academic, professor Mohan Rao, who teaches at the prestigious Jawaharlal Nehru University, said that the country was witnessing "reproductive trafficking," referring to the fact that most cash-strapped surrogate mothers are from rural India and travel to metropolitan centers to offer their services as a last-ditch effort to get money. This view is fiercely challenged by those who see surrogacy as a means to economic empowerment of women and as a decision women should be free to make for themselves.

But the usual empowerment vs. exploitation debate eludes something much more fundamental that the surrogate industry reflects about India. India has leap-frogged several stages of development and zoomed straight into a service economy. Indians stock call centers and tech help lines where Westerners can get their questions answered efficiently. In these centers, Indian youths temporarily adopt new personal identities by using Western names and accents—another, milder way that Indians act as "surrogates," or substitutes for Westerners. The country is romanced by the idea of selling human capital as its next great commodity. So surrogacy resonates not as an old problem of exploiting the poor but as an inevitable part of the "new India," where the locals provide much needed services for the new global economy. This kind of forward-thinking economic liberation dovetails with an ideology of personal freedom. "I think women should be free to choose what they do with their bodies," says Dr. Aniruddha Malpani, a fertility specialist in Mumbai. "We shouldn't treat them as stupid just because they are poor."

This appeal to modern ideals of self-determination make sense to members of the "new India" like Dr. Malpani and his clients. The problem is that the surrogates are not members of *this* India. Alan Greenspan writes that "India is fast becoming two entities: a rising kernel of world-class modernity within a historic culture that has been for the most part stagnating for generations." The surrogates tend to hail from this "historic culture," which is essentially semi-feudal and pre-industrial. It is this gap that allows for exploitation in surrogacy and other industries to happen, and it is the gap—not surrogacy itself— that is the root of the problem.

Perpetuating Social Inequality

To exercise one's freedom meaningfully requires information and education, and many surrogates are deeply ignorant about what the procedure entails. It is not uncommon for surrogates to authorize contracts with a thumbprint as opposed to a signature because they are illiterate. Even those who are literate often aren't able to read the contracts, which tend to be written in English. Lack of technological understanding among rural Indians also breeds misconceptions about surrogacy. Many, for example, thought that it would be necessary to sleep with another man in order to conceive. Even the pricing structure of surrogacy perpetuates social inequality: Many religious Indian surrogacy clients would prefer for their child to be birthed by an upper-caste *brahmin*, so high-born surrogates can get paid up to double.

These problems are hardly going to stop the phenomenon of surrogacy in India from spreading, though. In fact, one might even suggest that India is moving towards a surrogacy-based economy, in which Indians—in call centers and fertility clinics alike—specialize in substituting Westerners in a cheaper, more efficient way.

Government Policies Should Not Treat Women as Childbearing Vessels

Sunsara Taylor

Sunsara Taylor writes for Revolution Newspaper *and hosts* WBAI's Equal Time for Freethought *radio program. Her writing largely concerns war, the worldwide rise of theocracy, and repression in the United States.*

In April 2006 (during the second term of President George W. Bush), the Centers for Disease Control and Prevention released a report recommending that doctors consider treating all women of childbearing age as potentially pregnant and also calling for a media blitz advising all women to embrace good preconception health habits, including healthy diets and a limit on the use of caffeine, tobacco, alcohol, and other drugs. In the following viewpoint, Taylor asserts that this report treats women as though they are merely vessels, existing only to bear children. While some applauded these recommendations as representing good and reasonable health care, Taylor sees their potential to erode women's rights, setting the stage for repressive measures related to birth control, childbirth, and abortion.

Not planning on getting pregnant? The Centers for Disease Control and Prevention (CDC) doesn't care. As far as it is concerned, if you are one of the 62 million U.S. women of childbearing age, you are pre-pregnant—a vessel. You are a future fetal incubator.

In April [2006], the CDC issued a report detailing measures to be taken to intervene in the life, healthcare and behavior of all women, "from menarche [first occurrence of menstruation] to menopause . . . even if they do not intend to conceive."

Interfering in Women's Lives

The CDC report calls for a radical shift in medical care so that at every point of interaction, women's doctors are to stage "interventions" to make sure they are healthy and prepared to give birth. Want to take your newborn in for a checkup or your 8-year-old in for a high fever? Expect an "intervention" into your eating habits, weight and behavioral risk factors.

Got diabetes or epilepsy and looking for the care that is best for you? Wrong approach, says the CDC: "Separating childbearing from the management of chronic health problems and infectious diseases places women, their future pregnancies, and their future children at unnecessary risk."

Noting that attitudes and behavior related to childbearing and childbearing preparedness are "influenced by childhood experiences and prevailing social norms among adults," the CDC calls for a cultural and media crusade aimed at changing "public attitudes" about "the importance of preconception health behaviors," including the risks of tobacco use, alcohol, obesity, and diet.

The report bemoans the fact that half of all pregnancies are unplanned, and focuses in on the potential harm caused to fetuses by their female incubators between the time of an unexpected conception and the recognition of pregnancy. Never mind making it easier for women to decide for themselves whether or not to become pregnant. Never mind ensuring that women have the ability to terminate unwanted pregnancies. Not once, in its entire 43 pages, does the CDC's report even mention birth control or elective abortion.

Instead, the CDC report is framed in and extends the kind of logic that has galvanized the anti-abortion movement for years. Now, not only is the developing life of a fetus—a potential human being—considered more valuable and important than the life of the mother—but the potential life of a nonexistent fetus takes precedence over the life of the woman.

Women as Less Important than Fetuses

But what is a fetus? It is nothing more than a potential human being. And the only way it can grow into a human, a separate social being, is by being a subordinate part of a woman's body and her biological processes for months.

It is a very sobering sign of the times that there is so much confusion over the truth that a fully formed woman's life—and her will—is more valuable than this subordinate part of her own biology. Sobering, too, is the idea of the America we're headed for should we not see a huge outpouring of rage, furious resistance and indignant, uncompromising insistence that "Women are not incubators!"

Failing that, get prepared for the religious fanatics who terrorize women at the doors of abortion clinics to broaden their harassment against women who enter bars, smoke cigarettes or eat at McDonald's. Get ready for the prosecution of women who engage in these activities for crimes against their future fetuses. And get ready for calls to weed out and even sterilize women who are deemed by the state to be unfit to bear children.

A Cultural Shift Is Already Under Way

Sound too extreme? Wake up and look around!

- Already, legions of theocratic lawyers are constructing legal defenses for the fundamentalist pharmacists who refuse to fill women's prescriptions for birth control.
- Already, Louisiana has joined South Dakota in banning abortion throughout the state.

- Already, Sen. Tom Coburn (R-Okla.) and others have called for the execution of abortion providers.

- Already, laws passed to "protect" fetuses have been used to jail people who, lacking safe and destigmatized access to legal abortions, either self-induced an abortion or helped a woman induce her own voluntary abortion.

- Consider that the Rev. Thomas J. Euteneuer, the leader of Virginia-based Human Life International, has called the repressive anti-abortion laws in El Salvador "an inspiration." As *The New York Times Magazine* said in describing the situation in El Salvador: "In the event that the woman's illegal abortion went badly and the doctors have to perform a hysterectomy, then the uterus is sent to the Forensic Institute, where the government's doctors analyze it and retain custody of her uterus as evidence against her."

- And think what it means that the born-again commander in chief, [President] George W. Bush, has met with and lent political support to the "Snowflakes." The Snowflakes Frozen Embryo Adoption Program is a Christian conservative movement that finds women to act as incubators in an effort to bring to term every frozen embryo that would normally be discarded by fertility clinics. Then, in a sick and sinister fashion, they take the resulting babies and parade them around—including in photo ops such as one with President Bush—to crusade against stem cell research and to agitate for the position that a woman's primary function is to reproduce.

An Immoral Stance Against All Women

The CDC gives the appearance of being concerned about the high infant mortality rates among uninsured, poor and oppressed women. (And indeed, the need for concern is real: Mortality rates for infants born to black women in Brooklyn are comparable to the rates of many Third World countries.) Its report recommends intensive interventions into the lives of women who are at high risk, singling out race and economics as determining factors. But the "interventions" are not aimed at solving the conditions that cause women to be poor, to lack healthcare or to be trapped in abusive relationships. Instead, the report's recommendations lay a blueprint for exploiting these women's underprivileged conditions as a means of further intruding into, and even criminalizing, intimate aspects of their lives.

And when you get right down to it, this report has potentially genocidal implications. By formalizing the idea that certain women chronically put themselves at risk of being less-than-perfect potential mothers, the CDC paves the way for acceptance of the idea that certain women are unfit to reproduce.

Paranoia, you say? Let's not forget this country's long and shameful history of removing children from Native Americans who were deemed unfit to raise them. Or its history of forced sterilization of black and Puerto Rican women without healthcare who went to hospitals to give birth.

The CDC's report takes a viciously immoral stance toward half of humanity. It needs to be answered—by scientists and doctors refuting the bases of its recommendations; by social scientists and historians, bringing to light what has happened in places like Nazi Germany, where all young women were classified as breeders; and most of all by millions of outraged women and men who refuse to march forward into a real-life *Handmaid's Tale*.

Modesty Is Forced on Women in Chechnya

Tanya Lokshina

Tanya Lokshina is deputy director of the Moscow offices of Human Rights Watch and a frequent contributor to the Washington Post, *the* Guardian *(UK), and the Russian current affairs news site* Polit.ru. *Lokshina is also the author of the books* Chechnya Inside Out *and* Imposition of a Fake Political Settlement in the Northern Caucasus.

The Chechen Republic—which was formerly a part of the Soviet Union and is now a member of the Russian Federation—has been an almost entirely Sunni Muslim region for nearly four hundred years. Since the dissolution of the Soviet Union in the 1990s, the region has been unstable, with many violent conflicts between pro-Russian authorities and separatists. In 2010 Lokshina conducted a series of interviews with Chechen women in order to document a conservative cultural shift and its impact on the lives of women. According to the author, it is becoming increasingly difficult for Chechen women to move freely throughout their country and increasingly acceptable for men to publicly attack and humiliate women who they believe are not appropriately veiled, meek, and modest.

Even in the 90s at the time of the Chechen Republic of Ichkeria it wasn't as bad as it is now. After all I didn't wear a headscarf then and, though the keepers of public morals would sometimes pounce on you, they kept their hands to themselves. You could say to them 'What's it got to do with you? I've got a father and brothers, so who are you to give me orders?' They didn't want problems, so they'd back off. But now [2010] you don't know where to hide. They have the power and the strength and they're everywhere.

The pretty young woman in a straight, well-fitting skirt and crisp light-coloured blouse gestures helplessly.

It's so humiliating, but you have no other option—you have to put on the headscarf. If, say, they hit you, and that's not unlikely, then your brothers won't be able to leave it at that. They'll have to take action against the aggressors, who will just kill them. You dress according to their rules not so much out of fear for yourself, but to protect your family.

President Approves Attacks on Women

In June Madina and her friend were fired at from a paintball gun. At first they thought it was a real gun, even perhaps a sub-machine gun. They were walking along the main street in Grozny, talking and laughing. Suddenly a car with no number plates stopped beside them. The side window was wound down and the gun barrel appeared. The world suddenly shrank to the size of that barrel and was sucked into a black hole. Madina heard the shots, felt a sharp blow to her chest and pressed close to the wall of the house. She was sure she was dying, but for some reason she didn't lose consciousness and the stain spreading over her blouse was not red, but blue. The wall was blue too. The skirt of her friend, who was paralysed with fear, was stained green. She caught sight of a pudgy grinning face in the car window. The man was laughing and pointing at her. He had a powerful arm and she could see the black uniform of the "Kadyrovites", the president's men. She thought his laughter would burst her eardrums.

Madina felt the pain a bit later, though it was actually a feeling of intense burning, which then developed into pain. Her friend came to her senses first and, seizing Madina's hand, dragged her into the nearest shop. The sales assistant reacted with horror, clicking her tongue and trying to get the stains out with damp paper napkins. She massaged the bruises that were starting to spread and recommended putting ice on them when she got home. She called a taxi for the girls. It was while they were getting into it that they saw the splodges of red, blue and green paint on the pavement and the walls of the buildings. They realised that they had not been the only targets. On the road there were some yellow leaflets. Madina picked one up and only then grasped what this had actually all been about. The black letters danced before her eyes:

Dear Sisters!

We want to remind you that, in accordance with the rules and customs of Islam, every Chechen woman is OBLIGED TO WEAR A HEADSCARF.

Are you not disgusted when you hear the indecent 'compliments' and proposals that are addressed to you because you have dressed so provocatively and have not covered your head? THINK ABOUT IT!!!

Today we have sprayed you with paint, but this is only a WARNING!!! DON'T COMPEL US TO HAVE RECOURSE TO MORE PERSUASIVE MEASURES!!!

The next day Madina put on a headscarf. She saw no other solution. Every crossroad and every corner were unbearably frightening: she seemed to see men dressed in black, the enforcers of morality and the law. For another two weeks these men were actually driving around the city, patrolling the central streets. Women no longer went out with their heads uncovered—especially as President Kadyrov himself clearly supports attempts to inculcate female modesty. He even said on TV that if he found the men who had sprayed the girls with paint, he would offer them his thanks.

A Culture Shifting Against Women

By the middle of summer the peak seemed to have passed. True, rumours abounded that unmarried women would lose their jobs and not even be allowed to finish their university studies. But so far no one has been sacked, so perhaps these are only rumours. . . . Girls have once more started appearing in the city centre with short sleeves and their heads uncovered. You wouldn't go to school, the university or the office without a headscarf, but you could apparently pull it off when you're just walking along the street.

Ramadan [the Muslim holy month] started in the middle of August, and the main prospect was full of men. This time it wasn't secret service men, but people in Islamic clothing from the Centre of Spiritual and Moral Education affiliated to the Islamic High Council of Chechnya. They were distributing coloured folding leaflets to women, showing how Muslim women should be properly dressed. There was also a description of how a Chechen woman should look and behave. The authors' instructions to women read: *"Dear sister in Islam! Today Chechnya wants to uphold decency and morality. Your dress, dear sister, should be a demonstration of your purity and your morality, but mainly of your faith. Your clothes and your morality preserve your honour and that of your relatives and parents!"*

The leaflets also urged men to take charge of how their women looked: *"It has unfortunately to be admitted that a terrible picture is to be seen in the streets. We are not accusing women. The main fault is the men's. A woman won't lose her mind if her husband doesn't. Men, we need your help. Of all that we see, the worst is the way some women dress. But what is even more terrible is that the menfolk allow their sisters, wives and daughters to dress in this way and don't consider that it is wrong to do so."*

The morality zealots went around in groups. They surrounded women who had been bold enough to go out without a headscarf or in a skirt that was deemed too short. They upbraided them loudly, describing their behaviour as indecent and demanding that they should have some shame and "get dressed" forthwith.

Chechen students wearing Islamic headscarves during the newly established "Day of Chechen Women" in September 2010. In 2006 the Chechen government imposed a strict Islamic dress code on women, angering human rights groups around the world. © AP Photo/ Musa Sadulayev.

A Culture Shock for Other Russians

Yakhita didn't really understand what was going on. She had been living in Moscow for a long time, only coming home to Grozny [the Chechen capital] on holiday to see her family. She had, of course, noticed the prominence of headscarves: women reading the news on television, teachers, staff of various organisations, students, even girls in the first year of school had all suddenly put them on. Her friends talked quietly about how during the war [the First and Second Chechen Wars, both in the 1990s] men had not protested when women rescued them, protected them and worked until they dropped to feed the family. But now they've remembered they're men and that "a woman should know her place." Yakhita nodded in agreement, but only half listening. It wasn't her problem, when all's said and done. But it turned out that it was.

She was walking along the prospect carrying her newborn baby and pulling her 3-year-old son after her. It was very hot, so she had put on a knee-length skirt and a light T-shirt with short sleeves. She had actually put a hairband on—a headscarf folded over several times. Why not, really? Suddenly four men in Islamic clothing came up to her and started shouting, pointing at her bare arms and saying that she was behaving indecently and shamefully. Yakhita was so surprised, she was nearly at a loss for words.

But then she pulled herself together and started shouting that she was married with two children and had never in her whole life done anything shameful, so they had no right to make such comments. She repeated that she had a husband and a brother and that she would ring them up right now to come and sort things out. Seeing her reaching for her mobile, the men retreated. One of them said: "You don't need to ring anyone. Don't make a fuss. We have our orders from above. We've got to do this, do you understand?" Yakhita got the message and didn't want to stay any longer. The next day she bought her ticket back to Moscow.

Women Driven to Desperation

Zealots in Islamic clothing were soon joined by aggressive young men. Some of them went as far as grabbing girls by the arms and pulling their hair. Law enforcement officers also took up teaching women morality with great pleasure. Fatima is 19. Her mother implored her not to go out without a headscarf, especially in the city centre. "Don't provoke them, oh please don't! They might even kill you. Yesterday a girl was walking along in Chemorechye district without a headscarf. She was bundled into a car and driven off. No one knows where she is now!" Fatima put on a headscarf so as not to upset her mother, but when she got outside, she put it in her bag. It felt too humiliating to cover her head just because she'd been told to. This was the very beginning of the month of Ramadan. Her hair was loose and she had on a long, but fairly tight, dress. It was new and Fatima had been admiring it that morning in the mirror.

At the corner there were two cars of Kadyrov's men—young, bearded, in black uniforms and armed. There were about seven or eight of them. They shouted at the girl, obviously trying to strike up an acquaintance. She pretended she hadn't heard and started walking faster. The lads leapt out of the cars and rushed after her. They surrounded her and starting talking smut. She tried to tell them where to get off, yelling "Leave me alone!" Then they got even more worked up, saying that if she had been decently dressed and wearing a headscarf, no one would be pestering her. She was dressed in such a way as to attract men's attention and be a temptation to them. They told her she was a slut and belonged on the muck heap. They grabbed her hands and started dragging her toward the rubbish bin.

The girl was crying and trying to resist. She was being pulled by the hair. There were people in the street, but no one intervened. Only one woman of about 40 couldn't bear it any longer. She ran toward Fatima, grabbed hold of her and yelled: "What are you doing? Let the girl go!" The young men tried to shake her off, but she wouldn't let go and continued to shout even more loudly. Finally they let go of Fatima and left. The girl is still praying for her saviour, who doesn't herself understand how she didn't lose her nerve.

The woman probably lost her head. Her feelings of horror and pity were stronger than the instinct for self-preservation. She herself actually wears a headscarf, because she thinks it's right. She's been wearing it for many years, but now she sometimes wants to take it off: "You see, this kind of behaviour makes even a woman who wants to wear a headscarf start feeling that it's choking her."

For Further Discussion

1. Throughout her writing—including *The Handmaid's Tale*—Margaret Atwood has consistently argued for universal human rights, explicitly including the rights of women as full and equal citizens. She has defended freedom of speech (even as it applies to speech that she may personally find offensive, such as pornography) and unfettered access to abortion services. Many critics of Atwood, including Anne Barbeau Gardiner, argue that this puts Atwood—and women in general—on the wrong side of these arguments and that the continued existence of both abortion and pornography implicitly degrade women's status. Where would Offred stand in this debate? What about her mother? Moira? Having read *The Handmaid's Tale*, has your opinion of these kinds of freedom changed, or has it been reinforced? How?

2. Many critics point out that several of Atwood's novels—especially *The Robber Bride* and *Cat's Eye*—push one step beyond feminism, revealing women to be the victims not simply of patriarchy but also of each other. This same point, specific to *The Handmaid's Tale*, is made by Tara J. Johnson. Are the women in *The Handmaid's Tale* oppressing each other? More so than they are oppressed by men? And how does this play out in the real-world examples cited in the viewpoints by Amana Fontanella-Khan, Sunsara Taylor, and Tanya Lokshina? Is it telling, or simply coincidental, that the most scathing attacks on Atwood and her novel included in this volume have been written by women?

3. Reviewers often pigeonhole *The Handmaid's Tale* as a "feminist dystopia" or "feminist horror story." Atwood her-

self has characterized the novel as a cautionary tale and notes that it was inspired by 1970s and 1980s conservative political shifts she saw firsthand in the United States and Iran and that she read reports of throughout the world. In their viewpoints, Jill Swale, Shirley Neuman, Barbara Ehrenreich, and Tara J. Johnson all argue, at least in part, that the novel illustrates how postfeminist complacency—the assumption that women have "won" their rights and thus no longer need to worry about them—will almost inevitably lead to the erosion of those rights. Are there recent political developments or news items that lead you to believe that women's rights are being eroded? Conversely, does the recent prominence of female politicians and pundits—especially at the national level and among conservatives—prove that women have finally "made it"?

For Further Reading

Margaret Atwood, *The Blind Assassin: A Novel*. New York: Talese, 2000.

Margaret Atwood, *Oryx and Crake*. New York: Talese, 2003.

Margaret Atwood, *The Robber Bride*. New York: Talese/ Doubleday, 1993.

Margaret Atwood, *The Year of the Flood*. New York: Talese/ Doubleday, 2009.

Paolo Bacigalupi, *The Windup Girl*. San Francisco: Night Shade Books, 2009.

Jim Crace, *The Pesthouse*. New York: Talese, 2007.

Aldous Huxley, *Brave New World*. Garden City, NY: Doubleday, Doran and Co., 1932.

Laura Kasischke, *In a Perfect World: A Novel*. New York: HarperPerennial, 2009.

Ursula K. Le Guin, *The Left Hand of Darkness*. New York: Walker, 1969.

Cormac McCarthy, *The Road*. New York: Knopf, 2006.

George Orwell, *Nineteen Eighty-Four*. New York: Harcourt, Brace, 1949.

Joanna Russ, *The Female Man*. New York: Bantam, 1975.

Sheri S. Tepper, *Gibbon's Decline and Fall*. New York: Bantam, 1996.

James Tiptree, *Her Smoke Rose Up Forever: The Great Years of James Tiptree, Jr.* Sauk City, WI: Arkham House, 1990.

Kate Wilhelm, *Where Late the Sweet Birds Sang*. New York: Harper and Row, 1976.

Bibliography

Books

Margaret Atwood   *Negotiating with the Dead: A Writer on Writing.* New York: Cambridge University Press, 2002.

Margaret Atwood   *Payback: Debt and the Shadow Side of Wealth.* Toronto: House of Anansi Press, 2008.

Harold Bloom   *Margaret Atwood.* New York: Blooms Literary Criticism, 2009.

J. Brooks Bouson *Critical Insights: "The Handmaid's Tale".* Pasadena, CA: Salem Press, 2009.

Peter C.   *A History of the Birth Control*
Engelman   *Movement in America.* Santa Barbara, CA: Praeger, 2011.

Zara Griswold   *Surrogacy Was the Way: Twenty Intended Mothers Tell Their Stories.* Gurnee, IL: Nightengale Press, 2006.

Elaine Tyler May *America and the Pill: A History of Promise, Peril, and Liberation.* New York: Basic Books, 2010.

Ellen McWilliams *Margaret Atwood and the Female Bildungsroman.* Burlington, VT: Ashgate, 2009.

Johanna Schoen   *Choice and Coercion: Birth Control,*
                      Sterilization, and Abortion in Public
                      Health and Welfare. Chapel Hill:
                      University of North Carolina Press,
                      2005.

P.L. Thomas   *Reading, Learning, Teaching Margaret*
                      Atwood. New York: Peter Lang, 2007.

France   *Outsourcing the Womb: Race, Class*
Winddance Twine   *and Gestational Surrogacy in a Global*
                      Market. New York: Routledge, 2011.

Periodicals and Internet Sources

Mary Adams   "Rereading Atwood After the
                      Taliban," *World Literature Today,*
                      October 8, 2010.

Anonymous   *"The Handmaid's Tale," Heretical Sex*
                      (blog), July 8, 2006.
                      Hereticalsex.blogspot.com.

Gorman   "The Politics of *The Handmaid's*
Beauchamp   *Tale," Midwest Quarterly,* vol. 51, no.
                      1, 2009.

Rhys Blakely and   "'Rent-A-Womb' Baby Trade Faces
Rosemary Bennett   Curbs amid Fears for Surrogates,"
                      Times (London), March 15, 2008.
                      www.timesonline.co.uk.

Jess DelBalzo and   "Reproductive Exploitation," Keep
Bryony Lake   Your Baby, 2003. www.keepyour
                      baby.com.

Jonah Goldberg   "A Dark Past," *National Review,* June
                      24, 2008. www.nationalreview.com.

Paul Gray   "Review: *The Handmaid's Tale*," *Time*, February 10, 1986.

Chris Hedges   "The Christian Fascists Are Growing Stronger," Truthdig, June 7, 2010. www.truthdig.com.

Orrin Judd   "Review of Margaret Atwood's *The Handmaid's Tale*," BrothersJudd.com, April 24, 2003. www.brothers judd.com.

Ursula K. Le Guin Review of *The Year of the Flood*, by Margaret Atwood, *Guardian* (London), August 29, 2009. www.guardian.co.uk.

Joyce Carol Oates "Margaret Atwood's Tale," *New York Review of Books*, November 2, 2006.

January W. Payne "Forever Pregnant," *Washington Post*, May 16, 2006. www.washington post.com.

Shikha Prashad   "(Almost) Real Handmaids," *Gender and Technology Spring 2009* (blog), April 15, 2009. Gandt.blogs .brynmawr.edu.

Mervyn Rothstein "No Balm in Gilead for Margaret Atwood," *New York Times*, February 17, 1986.

Kristin Rushowy "Atwood Novel Too Brutal, Sexist for School," *Toronto Star*, January 16, 2009. www.thestar.com.

Kiran Shah   "Gandhi in *The Handmaid's Tale*,"
                      Chowk, October 4, 2005.
                      www.chowk.com.

Noreen Shanahan "Fighting Gender Apartheid in
                      Afghanistan," *Herizons*, Fall 1999.

Judith Sunderland "How Not to Liberate Women,"
                      Guardian (London), April 24, 2010.
                      www.guardian.co.uk.

Index